SOYFOOD RECIPES FOR THE AMERICAN TABLE

SOYFOOD RECIPES FOR THE AMERICAN TABLE

Favorite Dishes From the Folks at
White Wave

America's Soyfood Company Since 1977

Book Publishing Company
Summertown, Tennessee

Interior design: Warren C. Jefferson
Cover design: James Thurman
Graphic design: Randa Abbas

ISBN 1-57067-067-6

Published in the United States by
Book Publishing Company
P.O. Box 99
Summertown, TN 38483
888-260-8458
bookpubl@usit.net

1 2 3 4 5 6   00 99 98

Soyfood recipes for the American table / White Wave, Inc.
        p.   cm.
    Includes index.
    ISBN 1-57067-067-6 (alk. paper)
    1. Vegetarian cookery. 2. Soyfoods I. White Wave (Company)
TX837.S6855   1999
641.6'5655- -dc21   98-53286
                                                                     CIP

Some of the recipes in this book are taken from the following Book Publishing Company titles: *Tofu Cookery, Tofu Quick & Easy, Lighten Up!,* and *Soyfoods Cookery,* by Louise Hagler; *The Almost No-Fat Cookbook, The Almost No-Fat Holiday Cookbook,* and *20 Minutes to Dinner,* by Bryanna Clark Grogan; *The New Farm Vegetarian Cookbook,* ed. by Dorothy Bates and Louise Hagler; *Cooking with Gluten and Seitan,* by Dorothy Bates and Colby Wingate; *The Tempeh Cookbook,* by Dorothy Bates.

Calculations for the nutritional analyses in this book are based on the average number of servings listed with the recipes and the average amount of an ingredient, if a range is called for. Calculations are rounded up to the nearest gram. If two options for an ingredient are listed, the first one is used. Not included are optional ingredients, serving suggestions, or oil used for frying, unless the amount of oil is specified in the recipe.

CONTENTS

About White Wave • 7

About Soy • 9

About White Wave Products • 11

Breakfast • 15

Appetizers • 21

Soups • 27

Salads • 33

Main Dishes • 43

Desserts • 75

Index by Product • 87

General Index • 89

ABOUT WHITE WAVE

Entrepreneur Steve Demos founded White Wave, Inc., in 1977 as a "mom and pop" tofu shop, making tofu in a bathtub and delivering it locally to stores in a little red wagon. From these humble roots, White Wave has grown from a fledgling industry ahead of its time to one of the top producers of tofu and other soyfoods in North America and an innovator in the vegetarian foods market. With a pioneer's persistence, Demos and White Wave have nurtured the soyfoods market, creating and promoting products that at one time were bought only by hippies or health food "nuts," but now have become American household staples.

White Wave's reputation for quality, consistency, and innovation has led to a tremendous growth in sales of its soy products. This success has made Demos an award-winning entrepreneur and White Wave an award-winning business. Business acumen is only part of the story, as White Wave's founder believed in the concept of socially responsible living, "business without guilt," and "right livelihood" long before it was politically correct. It's this philosophy that has driven the company to pursue its goal of providing Americans with vegetarian products that are good for them and good for the planet. Offering over 50 vegetarian products, White Wave is dedicated to producing wholesome natural and organic foods made without artificial ingredients or additives.

White Wave's success has led Demos to be referred to as the "Soy Wonder" by *Entrepreneur Magazine* and "The King of Tofu" by the *Rocky Mountain News*. The *Boulder Daily Camera* dubbed Boulder "Tofu Town" due to White Wave's presence and its higher than average consumption of tofu and soy products. Employing over 75 people, White Wave's two Boulder, Colorado, facilities manufacture and distribute foods for the refrigerated sections of natural food stores and supermarkets throughout North America.

White Wave's mission is to creatively lead the full integration of healthy, natural vegetarian foods into the average American diet. "Our interest is in promoting the use of foods we consider the world better off with, rather than without, " states White Wave president Demos.

Healthy Soil Means Healthy Food

One reason White Wave has been supporting organic farming practices for over twenty years is because a naturally nourished soil does a better job producing vigorous plants than one boosted by artificial means. The soybeans White Wave uses in its products are grown without the use of synthetic pesticides, herbicides, or chemical fertilizers.

But more than that, White Wave believes in a farming philosophy that works with nature to produce strong, healthy crops without relying on chemicals. It's better for the Earth, it's better for the plants, and it's better for everyone.

Before crops can be certified organic, the land must be farmed this way for at least three years. Soybeans that are farmed using organic methods for less than three years are known as "transitionally grown" beans. When you purchase a transitionally grown product, you are supporting farmers making that three-year transition toward organic certification. And that increases the growth of organic farming in America. At White Wave, all soy products are made from certified organic soybeans or transitional soybeans.

ABOUT SOY

● Soybean protein provides all eight essential amino acids.

● Soy contains no cholesterol.

● It lowers the LDL ("bad") cholesterol without decreasing the HDL ("good") cholesterol.

● It's a great source of fiber.

● Soy may inhibit the activity of "cancer enzymes," enzymes that are much more active in cancer cells than in normal cells.*

● Soyfoods save water. Over half of all the water used in the United States is used for livestock production. In fact, it takes more water to produce a pound of beef than you would use taking a five-minute shower every weekday for a year.

*Messina, M. & Messina V. 1991. Increasing use of soyfoods and their potential role in cancer prevention. *J Am Diet Assoc.* 91:836-840.
Messina, M. & Barnes, S. 1991. The Role of Soy Products in Reducing Risk of Cancer. *J Nat Cancer Inst.* 83:541-546.

About White Wave Products

Several White Wave products are designed to be used right out of the package, such as Silk Dairyless Soy Yogurt and White Wave Silk Soymilk. Others, like White Wave Sandwich Slices and Soy A Melt, can be used just like their non-vegetarian counterparts.

Tofu

Tofu is one of the most versatile protein foods in the world. It is high in protein, relatively low in calories, fat, and carbohydrates, and contains no cholesterol. To make tofu, ground soybeans are simmered in water until the water becomes milky and flavorful. This "milk" is then curdled and pressed to form tofu. Tofu can be bought in several different forms, ranging from silken (the softest), to medium-soft, medium-firm, and hard-pressed, which is very dense and firm. Vacuum pack tofu is firmer than water pack; the vacuum process presses water out of the tofu, whereas tofu in a water pack absorbs water. Tofu will keep for up to one week if it is covered with water, stored in the refrigerator, and the water is changed daily. Plain tofu should have a fresh, mild flavor and aroma. If it smells "off" or sour, it has probably been mishandled and should not be eaten.

Firm tofu is best for slicing and cubing; soft tofu is best for blending and mashing. Both types are fine for crumbling. Substitute soft, blended tofu for sour cream in dips and spreads and in baked goods for part of the butter or oil to make your recipes lower in fat.

Tofu soaks up flavorful marinades more easily if some of the water it contains is pressed out first. To remove water from a block of tofu, wrap it in a clean dish towel and place a heavy plate or other weight on top for 20 minutes. Then slice or dice as needed. You can also squeeze the water out with your hands or wrap the block in a clean dish towel and twist at either end. This works best if you're going to crumble or mash the tofu anyway.

Some people like to slice and pan fry tofu in a little oil until it forms a golden skin before adding it to recipes. It will still absorb flavors and sauces, and it will hold together a little better than uncooked tofu.

You can freeze tofu to get a spongy, meat-like texture, perfect for use in pasta sauces or chili. Put an unopened package of tofu into the freezer, and keep it frozen at least 48 hours. Thaw at room temperature or immerse in hot water. The tofu will turn a creamy beige.

White Wave baked tofu is great either just out of the package or warmed. Also try it as a sandwich "meat," sliced over a salad, or wrapped in a tortilla or pita with your favorite vegetables.

If you're watching your calories, try White Wave's Fat-Reduced Tofu. A mechanical process is used to remove the fat rather than a chemical process.

Tempeh

Tempeh is a cultured food made by the controlled fermentation of soybeans and other grains and beans. The partially cooked beans (and sometimes grains) are mixed and incubated with rhizosporus oligosporus, a mold that grows delicate fibers that bind the beans and/or grains together to form a solid, sliceable cake. Fresh tempeh will have a nutty, mushroom-like aroma and flavor.

White Wave tempeh is pasteurized and ready to eat. Some individuals (particularly those just starting to eat tempeh) find tempeh easier to digest if it is cooked before eating.

Tempeh makes a good substitute for ground beef. In a food processor, chop the tempeh and use in spaghetti sauce, lasagne, etc. You can make it into "meatballs," or cube it and put it in soup, stews, and chilis.

Pan fry tempeh with a little oil and make a sandwich filling, or bake it with some cheese on top.

Tempeh is also good on the grill. Marinate it in soy sauce or barbecue sauce, and grill for about 3 minutes on each side, or skewer it on kabobs and grill with your favorite vegetables.

White Wave tempeh comes in several varieties—Original Soy, Wild Rice, Sea Veggie, Soy-Rice, and Five-Grain.

White Wave Silk Soymilk

White Wave Silk is a delicious soymilk that can be used in many of the same ways that one would use dairy milk. It will keep for about a week in the refrigerator. Freezing, however, will change the consistency and is not recommended. Silk can be used in hot beverages—try it foamed in a latte, or in hot chocolate. Silk Plain is good in soy-based cream soups and sauces. White Wave Silk is available in three varieties: Plain, Vanilla, and Chocolate.

White Wave Silk Dairyless Soy Yogurt

Silk Dairyless Soy Yogurt is a delicious way to enjoy the zesty flavors of yogurt without the problems associated with dairy products.

Soy A Melt

You can use White Wave Soy A Melt just as you would any dairy cheese: in sandwiches, salads, and as a topping for casseroles.

Seitan

Although seitan is not a soy product, it is becoming increasing popular as a meat substitute. It is made from gluten, the protein component of wheat. When gluten is cooked, it becomes seitan, a firm, sliceable food. Like tofu, seitan easily absorbs flavors from any herbs, spices, onions, or garlic you cook it with, and soy sauce and miso give seitan a rich, dark, beefy color. Seitan makes a delicious pot roast, and even a mock Thanksgiving "turkey." Also try it in pot pie, enchiladas and fajitas, ground in a food processor for chili or spaghetti sauce, and thinly sliced in a deli-style sub sandwich.

When heating seitan, either steam it in a little water or use another method that requires liquid (in a sauce or gravy), or sauté it in a little oil. Because seitan comes from just the protein in wheat, it contains no fat.

Breakfast

LIGHT AND EASY CORN MUFFINS

Yield: 12 muffins

Preparation Time: 10 to 15 minutes

Cooking Time: 20 minutes

These corn muffins are light and tender, with plenty of flavor. This is definitely "Yankee" corn bread on the sweet side. You can adjust the sugar to taste.

8 ounces *White Wave* **Reduced Fat Tofu**

½ cup water

⅓ cup sugar* or Sucanat, or ¼ cup honey

2 tablespoons nutritional yeast flakes

1 tablespoon lemon juice

⅞ cup unbleached white flour

¾ cup cornmeal

1 teaspoon baking soda

1 teaspoon baking powder

1 teaspoon salt

*If you prefer not to use sugar, replace the sugar or honey, water, and lemon juice with ½ cup thawed, frozen apple juice concentrate plus 3 tablespoons water

Preheat the oven to 350°F.

In a blender, mix the tofu, water, sugar, nutritional yeast, and lemon juice until very smooth.

In a medium bowl, mix together the flour, cornmeal, baking soda, baking powder, and salt.

Pour the blended mixture into the dry ingredients, and mix until they are just moistened. Spoon into 12 greased or nonstick muffin cups. (Paper muffin cups stick to very low-fat mixtures, so it's better not to use them.) Bake for 20 minutes. If you like a softer crust on your muffins, loosen them, turn them on their sides, and cover with a clean tea towel for 5 minutes while still hot from the oven.

For extra flavor, you can add 1 teaspoon cumin seeds, ½ cup steam-fried onions, 1 cup corn kernels, ¼ cup chopped green chilies, or 2 tablespoons soy bacon bits.

Per muffin: Calories 104, Total Protein 4 g, Soy Protein 2 g, Fat 1 g, Carbohydrates 20 g, Calcium 45 mg, Fiber 1 g, Sodium 249 mg

SCRAMBLED TOFU WRAP

Yield: 3 servings

Preparation Time: 10 minutes

Cooking Time: 5 minutes

Great for breakfast or any time you want an easy-to-make, neat-to-eat meal.
The vegetables listed are just a suggestion; experiment with your own favorites.

In a skillet, briefly sauté the garlic in the olive oil. Add the vegetables and sauté for a few more minutes. Add the tofu and stir until the tofu reaches the desired firmness. Spread ⅓ of the mixture down the center of each warmed tortilla, spoon on some salsa, fold, wrap, and GO!

1 clove garlic, minced

1 tablespoon olive oil

1 green bell pepper, chopped

1 red bell pepper, chopped

¼ cup chopped onion

4-5 mushrooms, sliced

1 pound *White Wave* Soft Tofu, drained and crumbled

3 large flour tortillas (burrito size works well)

¼ cup of your favorite salsa

Per serving: Calories 351, Total Protein 22 g, Soy Protein 17 g, Fat 18 g, Carbohydrates 28 g, Calcium 176 mg, Fiber 5 g, Sodium 424 mg

EGGLESS BLUEBERRY SOY MUFFINS

Yield: 12 muffins

Preparation Time: 10 minutes

Cooking Time: 20 minutes

Make these sweet, hearty muffins with either fresh or frozen blueberries. These muffins freeze well.

Dry Ingredients
¾ cup unbleached white flour

¾ cup whole wheat pastry flour

½ cup soy flour

¼ cup wheat germ

3 teaspoons baking powder

½ teaspoon salt

1½ cups *White Wave* Silk Soymilk

½ cup honey

2 tablespoons canola oil

1 teaspoon vanilla

1 cup fresh or frozen blueberries

Preheat the oven to 400°F.

Mix the dry ingredients together, and make a well in the middle.

Whip together the soymilk, honey, oil, and vanilla. Pour into the well in the dry ingredients, and stir just until blended. Fold in the blueberries, pour into oiled muffin tins, and bake for about 20 minutes until browned.

Per muffin: Calories 161, Total Protein 5 g, Soy Protein 3 g, Fat 4 g, Carbohydrates 27 g, Calcium 80 mg, Fiber 2 g, Sodium 103 mg

HERBED OATMEAL SCONES

Yield: 12 scones

Preparation Time: 10 to 15 minutes

Cooking Time: 15 to 20 minutes

Griddle breads are scones cooked on a griddle on top of the stove. This was the primary method of cooking in Ireland, Scotland, and Wales for centuries. These scones are moist and delicious, even without the modern addition of shortening.

Preheat the oven to 400°F.

Place the rolled oats in a dry blender or food processor, and whirl until the oats are ground to a fine meal. Pour them into a small bowl, and stir in the soymilk mixture. Add the herbs.

In a medium bowl, mix the flour, sugar, baking soda, and salt. Pour in the oat mixture, and mix briefly with a fork. Divide the dough in two. With wet hands, pat each half of the dough into an 8-inch circle in a lightly oiled or nonstick 9-inch cookie pan. Score each circle into 6 wedges. If you like, sprinkle the tops with caraway seeds. Bake for 15 to 20 minutes, or until golden, and serve hot.

Served for tea or breakfast, you can omit the herbs, split them with a fork, and spread them with jam or marmalade.

Variations

For a sweet scone, omit the herbs and sprinkle the tops with sugar before baking. You can also add ¼ cup dried currants or other dried fruit, if you like.

For Currant-Apple Scones, omit the herbs, use 3 tablespoons sugar in the dough, and add ½ cup dried currants and ¾ cup grated apple. Sprinkle the tops of the scones with sugar before baking.

1 cup rolled oats

1¼ cups *White Wave* Silk Soymilk mixed with

1 tablespoon lemon juice or vinegar

½ cup chopped and loosely packed fresh herbs of your choosing (parsley, chives, sage, savory, thyme, rosemary, etc.)

1¼ cups unbleached flour

1 teaspoon sugar or alternate sweetener

½ teaspoon baking soda

½ teaspoon salt

Caraway seeds for sprinkling on top (optional)

Per scone (with herbs): Calories 79, Total Protein 3 g, Soy Protein 1 g, Fat 1 g, Carbohydrates 14 g, Calcium 28 mg, Fiber 1 g, Sodium 133 mg

19

SOY CREPES

Yield: nine 10-inch crepes

Preparation Time: 5 minutes

Cooking Time: 10 minutes

These crepes can be enjoyed by themselves or as a versatile base for either savory or sweet fillings and sauces. Try them spread with jelly or applesauce or filled with scrambled tofu. Use them in place of noodles for manicotti.

½ cup unbleached white flour

½ cup whole wheat pastry flour

¼ cup soy flour

¼ cup nutritional yeast (optional)

½ teaspoon baking powder

½ teaspoon salt

3 cups *White Wave* Silk Soymilk

Mix the dry ingredients and make a well in the middle.

Pour in the soymilk and whip together. The batter should be very thin.

Heat a 10-inch nonstick crepe pan over moderate heat, and spray with nonstick spray. Pour in about ⅓ cup of the batter, tilting and moving the pan so that the batter covers the bottom of the pan with a thin coating. Cook until it is browned underneath and starts to pull away from the edge of the pan. Carefully flip it over and brown on the other side. Serve hot.

Per crepe: Calories 85, Total Protein 5 g, Soy Protein 3 g, Fat 1 g, Carbohydrates 13 g, Calcium 29 mg, Fiber 2 g, Sodium 152 mg

Appetizers

EGGLESS TOFU SALAD

Yield: about 3 cups (6 servings)

Preparation Time: 15 minutes

This versatile salad can make a sandwich, stuff a pita, top a bed of lettuce or tomato, or serve as a dip or spread with vegetables, chips, or crackers.

8 ounces *White Wave* Soft Tofu

3 tablespoons apple cider vinegar

1½ tablespoons sweetener of choice

1 teaspoon onion powder

1 teaspoon turmeric

½ teaspoon salt

½ teaspoon garlic powder

8 ounces *White Wave* Firm Tofu

½ cup chopped celery

½ cup finely grated carrot (optional)

½ cup chopped cucumber (optional)

¼ cup chopped onion

¼ cup chopped parsley

In a blender or food processor, blend the soft tofu, vinegar, sweetener, onion powder, turmeric, salt, and garlic powder until smooth.

Crumble the firm tofu into a bowl. Mix in the celery, carrot, cucumber, onion, and parsley. Stir in the blended tofu mixture, and serve.

Per ½ cup: Calories 197, Total Protein 8 g, Soy Protein 8 g, Fat: 5 g, Carbohydrates 6 g, Calcium 92 mg, Fiber 1 g, Sodium 193 mg

PHYLLO TRIANGLES WITH TEMPEH FILLING

Yield: 48 triangles
Preparation Time: 35 minutes
Cooking Time: 25 to 30 minutes

Flaky, fluffy hot appetizers that melt in your mouth.

Keep the filo leaves covered with a damp towel so they don't dry out. Steam the tempeh for 10 minutes, then cool and grate into a small bowl.

Sauté the onion and gingerroot in the oil until tender. Add the grated tempeh, tamari, garlic powder, oregano, allspice, and parsley. Stir together, then set aside to cool.

Open up 1 filo sheet, laying it flat on your work surface. Brush the sheet with melted margarine, fold in half, and brush again. Cut into 2-inch wide strips. Place a spoonful of filling at the edge of one end of the strip, and fold the corner over into a triangle. Keep folding the strip over into a triangle shape. Brush the top with margarine, and repeat this process with the other strips of filo.

These triangles can be covered and refrigerated or frozen for later baking. Preheat the oven to 400°F, and bake for 15 to 20 minutes, or until golden brown. Serve hot.

8 ounces unfrozen filo dough

8 ounces *White Wave* Organic Original Soy Tempeh

1 medium onion, finely chopped

1 teaspoon minced gingerroot

2 tablespoons oil

2 tablespoons tamari

½ teaspoon garlic powder

½ teaspoon oregano

¼ teaspoon allspice

2 tablespoons minced fresh parsley

¼ cup melted margarine

Per triangle: Calories 38, Total Protein 1 g, Soy Protein 1 g, Fat 2 g, Carbohydrates 4 g, Calcium 3 mg, Fiber 1 g, Sodium 70 mg

SPRING ROLLS

Yield: 10 servings
Preparation Time: 30 minutes
Cooking Time: 15 minutes

These can be rolled very thin for appetizers or thicker if part of a meal.

½ large cabbage
4 large carrots
1 large onion
2 green bell peppers
2 packages *White Wave*
  Chicken Style Seitan

5 cloves garlic, finely
  chopped
1 egg
Salt and pepper, to taste

20 spring roll or egg roll
  wrappers
Canola oil

Shred the cabbage, carrots, onion, peppers, and Chicken Style Seitan in a food processor. Place the shredded ingredients in a bowl, and add the garlic and egg. Mix well with your hands. Add the salt and pepper to taste.

Place ⅓ to ½ cup of the mixture in the center of a spring roll wrapper, spreading the filling diagonally from corner to corner. Fold over the 2 end corners to tuck around the filling. Then roll up from the bottom corner, and seal the edge with a little water. In a pan, heat enough oil to cover the rolls to 365°F. After the oil is hot (but not smoking), carefully place the rolls in the pan, and cook until they are brown. Carefully remove the rolls from the hot oil with a slotted spoon, and place them on paper towels. Serve with sweet and sour sauce.

Graciously shared by a long-time White Wave employee.

Per serving: Calories 185, Protein 9 g, Fat 5 g, Carbohydrates 26 g,
Calcium 44 mg, Fiber 4 g, Sodium 171 mg

STUFFED MUSHROOMS

Yield: 12 mushrooms

Preparation Time: 15 minutes

Cooking Time: 15 to 20 minutes

Mushrooms are full of flavor as well as vitamins and minerals, and there are only 90 calories in a whole pound. These can be served as an appetizer or entrée.

Clean the mushrooms by wiping with a damp cloth. Break off the stems and trim off the ends before chopping, setting the whole caps aside.

To make the filling, heat a skillet and add the olive oil, green onions, and chopped mushroom stems. Sauté for 3 minutes, then stir in the bread crumbs, seitan, marjoram, garlic powder, and a dash of salt and pepper. Cook for 2 minutes, mixing well.

Pack the filling in the cavities of the mushroom caps. Brush a skillet lightly with oil, and place the caps around the bottom, filled side up. Let the caps brown for a minute, reduce the heat, and add the stock to the bottom of the pan. Cover and simmer for 20 minutes.

You can also place the stuffed caps in a lightly oiled baking pan, add the stock, and bake uncovered at 375°F for 15 to 20 minutes.

12 large mushrooms

2 teaspoons olive oil

2 green onions, finely chopped

½ cup bread crumbs

½ cup *White Wave* Traditionally Seasoned Seitan

1 teaspoon marjoram

¼ teaspoon garlic powder

Dash of salt and pepper

½ cup vegetable stock

Per mushroom: Calories 30, Protein 2 g, Fat1 g, Carbohydrates 3 g, Calcium 7 mg, Fiber 0 g, Sodium 43 mg

Soups

MINESTRONE SOUP

Yield: 11 cups
Preparation Time: 20 minutes
Cooking Time: 45 minutes

1 pound *White Wave* Firm Tofu, frozen, thawed, squeezed dry, and cut into ¾-inch cubes
3 tablespoons tamari
½ teaspoon garlic powder

1 medium onion, chopped
2 carrots, sliced
1 medium zucchini, sliced
2 tablespoons olive oil

1 (28-ounce) can chopped tomatoes
4 cups water
2 cups tomato juice
2 teaspoons basil
½ teaspoon garlic powder
½ teaspoon salt
¼ teaspoon pepper
3 ounces noodles or broken spaghetti
1 (15-ounce) can kidney beans

Preheat the oven to 375°F.

MIx together the tamari and ½ teaspoon garlic powder, and squeeze into the tofu cubes. Place the cubes on an oiled cookie sheet, bake for 10 minutes, turn them over, and bake for 5 more minutes. Set aside.

Sauté the onion, carrots, and zucchini in the olive oil for about 10 minutes.

In a soup pot, combine the sautéed vegetables, tomatoes, water, tomato juice, basil, oregano, ½ teaspoon garlic powder, salt, and pepper, and bring to a boil.

Add the noodles, simmer for 15 minutes, then add the beans and tofu cubes. Serve when the beans are heated through.

Per cup: Calories 159, Total Protein 9 g, Soy Protein 5 g, Fat 5 g, Carbohydrates 19 g, Calcium 84 mg, Fiber 4 g, Sodium 521 mg

INDONESIAN CAULIFLOWER AND NOODLE SOUP

Yield: 8 servings
Preparation Time: 10 minutes
Cooking Time: 35 minutes

Cumin and coriander enhance the flavor of this savory dish.

Simmer the tempeh in the water for 15 minutes. Sauté the onion and garlic in the oil in a stock pot for 2 minutes. Add the cumin, coriander, cayenne, salt, vegetable stock, and cauliflower florets. Cover and simmer for 15 minutes. Add the noodles and cook until tender, about 6 to 8 minutes, adding the tempeh and its cooking liquid after 5 minutes. Transfer to a soup tureen, and sprinkle with the minced cilantro.

8 ounces *White Wave* Soy Rice Tempeh, cut into small cubes

1 cup water

1 small onion, chopped

2 cloves garlic, chopped

1 tablespoon oil

2 teaspoons cumin

1 teaspoon ground coriander

¼ teaspoon cayenne

1 teaspoon salt

1 quart vegetable stock

1 pound cauliflower, cut into florets

4 ounces fresh Chinese noodles or soba (thin Japanese buckwheat noodles)

2 tablespoons minced fresh cilantro (Chinese parsley)

Per serving: Calories 135, Total Protein 7 g, Soy Protein 1 g, Fat 4 g, Carbohydrates 19 g, Calcium 28 mg, Fiber 3 g, Sodium 275 mg

29

TEMPEH CHILI

Yield: 6 servings
Preparation Time: 30 minutes
Marinating Time: 1 hour
Cooking Time: 45 minutes

Marinade

2 tablespoons tamari

2 tablespoons water

¼ teaspoon garlic powder

¼ teaspoon onion powder

1 tablespoon soy or sesame oil

1 package *White Wave* Organic Original Soy Tempeh

1 tablespoon chili powder

1 teaspoon mustard powder or seed

1 teaspoon cumin

½ teaspoon oregano

6 tablespoons olive oil

1 onion, chopped

1 green bell pepper, chopped

1 teaspoon salt

¼ teaspoon black pepper

2 tablespoons tamari

1 tomato, chopped

1 (25-ounce) can whole peeled tomatoes, chopped (with juice)

1 (15-ounce) can kidney beans (plus juice and enough water to make 1 cup liquid)

Combine the marinade ingredients and mix well. Marinate the tempeh in the marinade for 1 hour, turning the tempeh over in the marinade after 30 minutes. Grate the tempeh and set aside with the marinade.

In a large saucepan, heat the chili powder, mustard, cumin, and oregano in the olive oil. Add the onion, green pepper, tempeh, and marinade, and sauté for a few minutes.

Add the rest of the ingredients, bring to a boil, lower the heat, and simmer for 30 minutes. Serve hot topped with grated cheese.

Per serving: Calories 347, Total Protein 16 g, Soy Protein 8 g, Fat 18 g, Carbohydrates 29 g, Calcium 64 mg, Fiber 10 g, Sodium 1039 mg

VEGETABLE SOUP PROVENÇALE

Yield: 6 servings
Preparation Time: 15 minutes
Cooking Time: 40 to 45 minutes

A nourishing soup that may simmer on the stove all day in a French farm house.

Simmer the potatoes and carrots in the boiling water, covered, for 15 minutes. Sauté the onions and cubed tempeh in the olive oil in a large stock pot for a few minutes, then add the cabbage and celery, and sauté over medium heat for 10 minutes. Add the potatoes and carrots with their cooking water, along with the vegetable stock, chopped tomatoes, garlic powder, thyme, and oregano. Bring to a boil. Cover the pan, turn the heat to low, and simmer the soup for 20 to 25 minutes. Add salt to taste. Just before serving, add the parsley.

3 potatoes, peeled and diced
2 large carrots, sliced
2 cups boiling water
2 large onions, chopped
8 ounces *White Wave* Five Grain Tempeh, cut in small cubes
2 tablespoons olive oil
½ head cabbage, shredded
2 ribs celery, thinly sliced
4 cups vegetable stock
1 (16-ounce) can chopped tomatoes
1 teaspoon garlic powder
½ teaspoon thyme
½ teaspoon oregano
¼ cup chopped fresh parsley

Per serving: Calories 220, Total Protein 8 g, Soy Protein 6 g, Fat 6 g, Carbohydrates 32 g, Calcium 71 mg, Fiber 7 g, Sodium 38 mg

31

Color photos, next two pages:
Spring Rolls, page 22
Tabouli, page 37

Salads

Color photos, previous two pages:
Chili Con Tofu With Beans, page 44
Lasagne with Tofu, page 47

GREEK SALAD

Yield: 10 to 12 servings
Preparation Time: 15 minutes
Marinating Time: 1 hour

Dressing
¼ cup olive oil
2 teaspoons wine vinegar
1 teaspoon salt
1 teaspoon basil
½ teaspoon black pepper
½ teaspoon oregano

1 pound *White Wave* Firm
Tofu, cut into ¾-inch cubes

3 tomatoes, cored and cut
into wedges
3 cucumbers, thinly sliced
½ large red onion, chopped
½ cup Greek or black olives
1 head leaf lettuce, washed,
dried, and separated

Combine the dressing ingredients, and pour over the tofu cubes. Marinate for at least 1 hour, stirring occasionally.

Add the tomatoes, cucumbers, onion, and olives to the marinated tofu. Toss and serve on the lettuce.

Variation
Substitute ½ pound feta for ½ pound of the tofu.

Per serving: Calories 118, Total Protein 5 g, Soy Protein 5 g, Fat 9 g,
Carbohydrates 5 g, Calcium 75 mg, Fiber 2 g, Sodium 250 mg

PICNIC POTATO SALAD

Yield: 6 to 8 servings
Preparation Time: 20 minutes
Cooking Time: 15 minutes
Chilling Time: 1 to 2 hours

Boil the potatoes in salt water until tender. Drain and pull the skins off.

Combine 1 tablespoon oil, 1 tablespoon vinegar, the salt, black pepper, and mustard, and add to the potatoes while still hot. Let cool.

Add the onion, celery, parsley, and celery salt to the cooled potato mixture.

Combine the dressing ingredients in a blender or food processor until smooth and creamy. Mix with the potatoes, chill, and serve.

4 medium potatoes, scrubbed well and cut into large chunks
1 tablespoon oil
1 tablespoon vinegar
½ teaspoon salt
⅛ teaspoon black pepper
⅛ teaspoon dry mustard

⅓ cup minced onion
1 cup diced celery
2 tablespoons minced fresh parsley
Celery salt, to taste

Dressing
¾ cup mashed *White Wave* Soft Tofu
2 tablespoons vinegar
1 tablespoon oil

Per serving: Calories 130, Total Protein 4 g, Soy Protein 3 g, Fat 6 g, Carbohydrates 17 g, Calcium 40 mg, Fiber 2 g, Sodium 169 mg

SPINACH-PINE NUT SALAD

Yield: 2 quarts (8 servings)
Preparation Time: 15 to 20 minutes

A glass bowl shows off the red and green of this colorful salad.

8 ounces *White Wave* Firm
Tofu, cut in small cubes

Dressing
2 tablespoons olive oil
2 tablespoons canola oil
2 tablespoons red wine
   vinegar
½ teaspoon salt
½ teaspoon dry mustard
¼ teaspoon black pepper

8 ounces young spinach
   leaves, washed and stems
   removed
1 small red onion, sliced
2 ribs celery, sliced on the
   diagonal
½ cup pine nuts

Place the tofu cubes in a glass serving bowl.

Combine the dressing ingredients in a small jar, and shake well to combine. Pour the dressing over the tofu cubes, and toss to coat. Add the remaining salad ingredients, and toss to mix well.

Per serving: Calories 150, Total Protein 6 g, Soy Protein 3 g, Fat 12 g,
Carbohydrates 3 g, Calcium 69 mg, Fiber 3 g, Sodium 168 mg

TABOULI

Yield: 6 cups (12 servings)
Preparation Time: 15 minutes
Cooking Time: 5 minutes
Soaking Time: 1 hour

Pour the boiling water into the bulgur, and stir well. Soak for 1 hour, then drain.

Add the remaining ingredients and mix well. Serve on a bed of leaf lettuce garnished with tomato wedges.

2 cups boiling water
1 cup bulgur wheat

1 cup finely chopped fresh parsley
½ cup finely chopped fresh mint
8 ounces *White Wave* Firm Tofu, finely chopped
2 tomatoes, chopped
½ cup black olives, chopped
¼ cup fresh lemon juice
¼ cup chopped scallions
2 tablespoons olive oil
½ teaspoon salt
¼ teaspoon black pepper

Per ½ cup serving: Calories 113, Total Protein 4 g, Soy Protein 2 g, Fat 5 g, Carbohydrates 14 g, Calcium 43 mg, Fiber 2 g, Sodium 138 mg

TACO SALAD

Yield: 4 quarts (8 servings)
Preparation Time: 20 minutes
Cooking Time: 5 minutes

1 pound *White Wave* Baked Tofu Jalapeño Mexican Style
or
1 pound *White Wave* Firm Tofu plus 1 (1¾-ounce) package taco seasoning mix
2 tablespoons oil

2 tomatoes, chopped
1 small head of lettuce, torn in bite size pieces
1 small onion, chopped
1 ripe avocado, cubed
1 cucumber, chopped
½ cup black or green olives, chopped

8 ounces corn chips

Crumble the Mexican-Style tofu into a bowl. (If using the plain tofu, crumble into a bowl, sprinkle with the seasoning mix, and mix together.) Heat the oil in a frying pan over medium heat, add the tofu mixture, and sauté until brown.

Arrange the tomatoes, lettuce, onion, avocado, cucumber, and olives in a large salad bowl. Right before serving, toss with the baked tofu and corn chips. Serve immediately so the chips won't get soggy. Serve with salsa on the side.

Per serving: Calories 357, Total Protein 15 g, Soy Protein 13 g, Fat 22 g, Carbohydrates 24 g, Calcium 73 mg, Fiber 4 g, Sodium 310 mg

TOFU PASTA SALAD

Yield: 6 servings
Preparation Time: 20 minutes
Cooking Time: 12 minutes

Add your favorite vegetables to this delightful, cool salad.

Cook the pasta according to package directions. While the pasta is cooking, briefly steam the vegetables until just slightly soft. Drain the pasta and combine with the vegetables and tofu. Combine the dressing ingredients, mix well, and stir into the salad mixture. Chill.

Contributed by a longtime White Wave employee.

1 (8-ounce) package spiral pasta
1 green bell pepper, diced
1 red bell pepper, diced
1 carrot, diced
1 small cauliflower, diced
2 stalks celery, diced
½ cup sweet peas
1 package *White Wave* Firm Tofu, cut into ½-inch cubes

Dressing
About ½ cup olive oil
About ½ cup vinegar
Salt and ground pepper, to taste
⅛ cup chopped fresh parsley

Per serving: Calories 326, Total Protein 12 g, Soy Protein 8 g, Fat 22 g, Carbohydrates 20 g, Calcium 112 mg, Fiber 4 g, Sodium 37 mg

SPINACH MUSHROOM SALAD

Yield: 6 servings

Preparation Time: 20 to 25 minutes

Cooking Time: 20 minutes

A classic salad, high in protein with the addition of tempeh.

8 ounces *White Wave* Soy Rice Tempeh

1 pound fresh spinach, well washed, stems discarded

1 small head Boston lettuce

2 tablespoons oil

1 clove garlic, cut in half

Dressing

Juice of one lemon

¼ cup olive oil

2 teaspoons brown rice syrup

½ teaspoon salt

½ teaspoon oregano

¼ teaspoon dry mustard

1 small red onion, thinly sliced and separated into rings

¼ pound mushrooms, thinly sliced

Steam the tempeh for 20 minutes; set aside to cool. Tear up the spinach and lettuce leaves, and set aside.

Dice the tempeh into small pieces, and fry in the 2 tablespoons oil. Rub a salad bowl with the cut garlic, then combine the lemon juice, ¼ cup olive oil, rice syrup, salt, oregano, and dry mustard to make a dressing. Combine the lettuce and tempeh with the sliced onions and mushrooms in the salad bowl, and toss gently with the dressing. Serve at once.

Per serving: Calories 225, Total Protein 8 g, Soy Protein 6 g, Fat 14 g, Carbohydrates 13 g, Calcium 99 mg, Fiber 6 g, Sodium 239 mg

CHICKEN-STYLE SALAD

Yield: 6 servings

Preparation Time: 10 minutes

Marinating Time: 1 hour

Deceptively simple, this fabulous salad can be enjoyed on a bed of lettuce or as a sandwich filling.

Combine the lemon thyme and mayonnaise, place in a covered container, and refrigerate for at least 1 hour. Combine with all of the remaining ingredients, mix, and add salt to taste.

¾ cup soy mayonnaise

½ teaspoon chopped fresh lemon thyme

1 (18-ounce) package *White Wave* Chicken Style Seitan, chopped into bite-size pieces

1 medium stalk celery, diced

5 green onions, sliced

5 teaspoons capers

5 sweet red bell peppers, diced

3 tablespoons chopped fennel

2 ounces pecans, chopped

Salt, to taste

Per serving: Calories 248, Protein 16 g, Fat 12 g, Carbohydrates 17 g, Calcium 62 mg, Fiber 9 g, Sodium 676 mg

ORIENTAL PASTA SALAD WITH PEANUT SAUCE

Yield: 4 servings

Preparation Time: 15 minutes

Cooking Time: 15 minutes

Chilling Time: overnight

This dish will provide a wonderful introduction to udon noodles,
an Oriental pasta similar in shape to linguine.

1 (8.8-ounce) package udon noodles or linguine

1 cup broccoli flowers and stems, cut in bite-size pieces

1 medium carrot, cut in matchsticks

8 ounces *White Wave* Baked Tofu Sesame Peanut Thai Style, cut in bite-size pieces (2 cups)

½ medium red bell pepper, cut in small strips

¼ cup toasted sesame seeds*

Peanut Sauce

½ cup warm water

2 tablespoons peanut butter

2 tablespoons tamari

2 tablespoons sesame or corn oil

1 tablespoon brown rice vinegar

½ teaspoon ground ginger

¼ teaspoon cayenne pepper

2 cloves garlic, pressed

Cook the noodles according to the package directions. Drain, rinse in cold water, and set aside in a large bowl.

Blanch the broccoli and carrot until bright in color, about 3 to 5 minutes. Add the vegetables, tofu, red pepper, and sesame seeds to the noodles, and combine.

To make the peanut sauce, mix the sauce ingredients in a suribachi (Japanese mortar and pestle), or in a Western-style mortar and pestle or blender.

Pour the sauce over the noodle mixture, and let set overnight in the refrigerator. Serve chilled.

* The sesame seeds can be toasted until light brown and aromatic by stirring in a dry skillet over medium heat or in a toaster oven. Watch carefully so they do not burn.

Per serving: Calories 475, Protein 26 g, Fat 18 g, Carbohydrates 50 g, Calcium 136 mg, Fiber 4 g, Sodium 1426 mg

Main Dishes

CHILI CON TOFU WITH BEANS

Yield: 1½ quarts
Preparation Time: 20 minutes
Cooking Time: 30 minutes

Tofu Marinade
¼ cup water
2 tablespoons tamari
1 tablespoon peanut butter
1 teaspoon onion powder
½ teaspoon cumin
¼ teaspoon garlic powder

1 pound *White Wave* Firm
  Tofu, frozen, thawed,
  squeezed dry, and torn into
  bite-size pieces

2 tablespoons oil

1 large green bell pepper,
  diced
1 large onion, diced
2 cloves garlic, minced

2½ cups cooked pinto beans
1 tablespoon chile powder
1 teaspoon cumin
1 teaspoon salt

Preheat the oven to 350°F.

Combine the tofu marinade ingredients, pour over the tofu pieces, and squeeze in so all of the liquid is evenly absorbed. Place the tofu pieces on a cookie sheet spread with 1 tablespoon of the oil, and bake for 20 minutes. Flip them over and bake for 10 more minutes. Remove from the oven and set aside.

In a heavy soup pot, sauté the green pepper, onion, and garlic in the remaining tablespoon of oil until tender. Add the tofu and all of the remaining ingredients, bring to a simmer, and serve hot.

Per serving: Calories 244, Total Protein 15 g, Soy Protein 9 g, Fat 11 g, Carbohydrates 23 g, Calcium 129 mg, Fiber 5 g, Sodium 701 mg

FRESH SHIITAKE STIR-FRY

Yield: 4 servings
Preparation Time: 15 minutes

Chop the ginger and garlic in a food processor. Add the mirin and tamari, and blend. Pour over the tofu, and let it marinate while preparing the vegetables.

Heat the oil in a wok, add the scallions and pepper, and stir-fry 1 minute. Add the mushrooms and snow peas, and stir-fry one minute. Add the tofu and the marinade, and stir-fry one more minute. Cover and steam until hot. Serve over brown rice.

1-inch cube fresh gingerroot, peeled

2 cloves garlic

¼ cup mirin

2 tablespoons tamari

1 pound *White Wave* Firm Tofu, cut into ½-inch cubes

½ cup sliced scallions

1 red bell pepper, cut into triangles

3½ ounces fresh shiitake mushrooms, sliced

8 ounces snow peas, washed and stems removed

1 tablespoon oil

Per serving: Calories 211, Total Protein 15 g, Soy Protein13 g, Fat 11 g, Carbohydrates 11 g, Calcium 162 mg, Fiber 5 g, Sodium 519 mg

HAWAIIAN STICKY TOFU

Yield: 4 servings
Preparation Time: 10 to 15 minutes
Cooking Time: 15 minutes

Serve this with steamed rice and raw vegetables for a kid-pleasing meal.
Leftovers are delicious cold!

¾ pound *White Wave*
Reduced Fat Tofu, cut into
16 slices

Sauce
6 tablespoons tamari
2 green onions
1 large clove garlic, peeled
1 teaspoon cornstarch
¾ teaspoon agar powder, or
1½ tablespoons agar flakes
½ cup plus 2 tablespoons
hot water
¼-⅓ cup liquid sweetener
1½ teaspoons chicken-style
broth powder
½ teaspoon each powdered
ginger and ground mustard
powder

1 (14-19-ounce) can
pineapple chunks, drained
1 large green or red bell
pepper (or ½ of each),
seeded and cut into
squares

Preheat the oven to 500°F. Quickly fry the tofu slices in a nonstick pan until browned on both sides. Place in one layer in a nonstick or lightly oiled 9 x 13-inch baking pan.

Place the tamari, green onion, garlic, cornstarch, and agar in a blender, and combine well. Add the remaining ingredients except the pineapple and green pepper. Mix well, then pour into a saucepan, and stir over high heat until it boils. Stir and continue to simmer for about 1 minute. Add the pineapple and green pepper, then pour over the tofu in the pan. Bake for 15 minutes.

Per serving: Calories 255, Total Protein 13 g, Soy Protein 12 g, Fat 4 g,
Carbohydrates 42 g, Calcium 66 mg, Fiber 3 g, Sodium 1571 mg

LASAGNE WITH TOFU

Yield 8 servings
Preparation Time: 25 minutes
Cooking Time: 50 minutes

Press the tofu to remove excess water by wrapping in a clean towel and placing a heavy pan on top for 10 to 15 minutes. After the tofu is pressed, combine it with the oil, lemon juice, salt, oregano, and basil in a food processor or with a potato masher. Cook the lasagne noodles until tender but firm.

Preheat the oven to 350°F. Lightly oil a 9 x 13-inch casserole or baking pan. Cover the bottom of the dish with a third of the sauce. Add ⅓ of the noodles, and spread with half the tofu mixture and half of the remaining sauce. Add another third of the noodles, the remaining tofu, the remaining noodles, then the remaining sauce. Top with the grated mozzarella and black olives, if desired. Cover the pan and bake for 20 minutes, then bake 20 more minutes uncovered.

1½ to 2 pounds *White Wave* **Firm Tofu**
¼ cup olive oil
⅛ cup fresh lemon juice
1 teaspoon salt
1 teaspoon oregano
2 tablespoons fresh minced basil, or 2 teaspoons dried basil
8 ounces lasagne noodles (9 large)
1 (32-ounce) jar Italian-style tomato sauce
1 cup grated soy or dairy mozzarella

⅓ cup black olives, sliced, for garnish (optional)

Per serving: Calories 396, Total Protein 27 g, Soy Protein 20 g, Fat 18 g, Carbohydrates 35 g, Calcium 244 mg, Fiber 8 g, Sodium 429 mg

47

LEMON GINGER TOFU OR TEMPEH

Yield: 8 slices (4 servings)
Preparation Time: 10 minutes
Marinating Time: 2 to 24 hours
Cooking Time: 5 to 10 minutes

Enjoy the zest of lemon and ginger.

2 tablespoons fresh lemon juice
½ tablespoon organic lemon zest
2 tablespoons tamari
1 tablespoon grated onion
1 clove garlic, pressed
½ tablespoon grated fresh gingerroot
1 pound *White Wave* Firm Tofu, cut in 8 slices
2 teaspoons sesame seeds

Mix together the lemon juice, zest, tamari, onion, garlic, and gingerroot. Arrange the tofu slices in one layer in a glass or stainless pan. Pour the lemon mixture over the tofu, and marinate from 2 to 24 hours.

Broiler Method: Preheat the broiler. Sprinkle the tofu slices with the sesame seeds, and broil 4 to 5 minutes until browned.

Stovetop Method: Brown the tofu slices on both sides in a small amount of soy or olive oil. Sprinkle with sesame seeds and serve.

Variation

Replace the tofu with 1 pound *White Wave* Soy Rice Tempeh that has been steamed for 20 minutes, and cut into ½-inch slices.

Per serving (tofu): Calories 130, Total Protein 14 g, Soy Protein 13 g, Fat 8 g, Carbohydrates 3 g, Calcium 144 mg, Fiber 1 g, Sodium 511 mg
Per serving (tempeh): Calories 228, Total Protein: 19 g, Soy Protein: 19 g, Fat: 9 g, Carbohydrates: 21 g, Calcium: 49 mg, Fiber 8 g, Sodium: 510 mg

MATTAR TOFU

Yield: 4 servings
Preparation Time: 15 minutes
Cooking Time: 10 to 15 minutes

One of the best-loved Indian restaurant dishes is mattar panir, a tomato-flavored mixture of green peas and cubes of fresh cheese. Firm tofu makes an excellent substitute for the cheese. Serve this with rice for a complete meal.

Dry-fry the tofu cubes in a large, non-stick skillet over high heat until they are golden on two sides. Remove from the pan and set aside.

Add the ginger and garlic to the hot pan, and steam-fry over high heat with a little bit of water for a minute. Add the onion and steam-fry until it is soft, about 5 minutes. Add the seasonings and ¼ cup water or broth, stirring well, then add the tomatoes, peas, tofu, and sweetener, and simmer 10 minutes. Serve over basmati or other rice.

¾ pound *White Wave* **Reduced Fat Tofu, cut into ½-inch cubes**

2 tablespoons grated fresh gingerroot, or 1 teaspoon powdered ginger

1 tablespoon chopped fresh garlic

1 medium onion, minced

1 tablespoon garam masala or curry powder

1 teaspoon salt

1 teaspoon turmeric

1 teaspoon ground coriander

Pinch cayenne

1 (14-ounce) can diced tomatoes with juice

1½ cups frozen baby peas (petit pois)

1 teaspoon liquid sweetener, sugar, or alternate

Per serving: Calories 182, Total Protein 13 g, Soy Protein 9 g, Fat 4 g, Carbohydrates 23 g, Calcium 99 mg, Fiber 7 g, Sodium 552 mg

OVEN FRIED TOFU

Yield: 4 to 6 servings
Preparation Time: 10 minutes
Cooking Time: 15 minutes

A quick and easy basic, this is one of our kids' favorites, delicious hot or cold.
Serve it with steamed grains and vegetables or in a sandwich with all the fixings.

1 pound *White Wave* Firm Tofu

6 tablespoons unbleached white or whole wheat flour

3 tablespoons nutritional yeast

2 teaspoons onion powder

1 teaspoon garlic powder

½ teaspoon poultry seasoning

¼ teaspoon freshly ground black pepper

1 tablespoon tamari

1 tablespoon oil

Preheat the oven to 400°F.

Slice the tofu ⅛ to ¼ inch thick.

Mix together the dry ingredients.

Dip the tofu in the tamari, then dredge in the flour mixture. Arrange on an oiled cookie sheet, and bake 10 minutes until browned on the bottom. Turn and bake about 5 more minutes until browned on the other side.

Variation

For a crunchier breading, replace the flour with finely ground cornmeal.

Oven Fried Chipotle Tofu

Replace the poultry seasoning and black pepper with ¼ teaspoon ground chipotle.

Per serving: Calories 160, Total Protein 14 g, Soy Protein 10 g, Fat 9 g, Carbohydrates 9 g, Calcium 124 mg, Fiber 2 g, Sodium 213 mg

SAVORY TOFU SPAGHETTI BALLS

Yield: sixteen 1½-inch balls
Preparation Time: 15 minutes
Baking Time: 30 minutes

Preheat the oven to 350°F.

Mix all the ingredients together, except the olive oil. Spread an 8 x 8-inch pan with the oil. Form the mixture into sixteen 1½-inch balls, and arrange in the pan. Bake about 30 minutes, or until browned and set, turning carefully about every 10 minutes.

1 pound *White Wave* Firm Tofu, mashed
½ cup wheat germ
¼ cup chopped parsley
2 tablespoons soy sauce
2 tablespoons nutritional yeast (optional)
1 tablespoon onion powder
½ teaspoon garlic powder
¼ teaspoon black pepper
¼ teaspoon oregano
2 tablespoons olive oil

Per ball: Calories 58, Total Protein 4 g, Soy Protein 3 g, Fat 3 g,
Carbohydrates 2 g, Calcium 33 mg, Fiber 1 g, Sodium 78 mg

SIZZLING SAVORY TOFU STEAKS

Yield: 3 servings
Preparation Time: 5 minutes
Cooking Time: 10 minutes

1 pound *White Wave* Firm
Tofu
3 tablespoons tamari
1 teaspoon garlic powder
1 teaspoon ground ginger
(optional)
1 tablespoon vegetable oil

Slice the tofu into "steaks" 2 x 3 x ½-inches. In a small bowl, whisk together the tamari, garlic, and ginger. Heat the oil in a skillet. Dip the tofu slices into the tamari mixture, and sauté over medium-high heat for 5 minutes. Flip and cook for 5 more minutes, or until browned on both sides.

Serve with green salad and baked potato.

Per serving: Calories 201, Total Protein 18 g, Soy Protein 18 g, Fat 14 g, Carbohydrates 3 g, Calcium 170 mg, Fiber 2 g, Sodium 1022 mg

SPAGHETTI PRIMAVERA

Yield: 4 to 6 servings
Preparation Time: 20 minutes
Marinating Time: 2 hours

Combine the tofu and marinade, and marinate for at least 2 hours. Brown the tofu in 1 tablespoon oil and the leftover marinade. Set aside.

In 1 inch of water, boil the broccoli and peas until almost tender. Drain and reserve the water.

Sauté the mushrooms in 1 tablespoon oil.

Cook the noodles until tender, and drain.

To make the sauce, combine ⅓ cup oil and the flour, and let bubble together over low heat for 3 minutes. Whisk in the 3 cups liquid without making lumps. Add the parsley, salt, garlic powder, and cayenne. Continue cooking over low heat, stirring until thickened and smooth.

Add the tofu, vegetables, and mushrooms to the sauce, and serve hot over the noodles.

Marinade
2 tablespoons tamari
2 tablespoons wine vinegar
1 tablespoon oil

1 pound *White Wave* Firm Tofu, cut into 2 x ½ x ⅛-inch pieces
1 tablespoon oil

4 cups fresh or frozen broccoli florets
1½ cups fresh or frozen peas
1 cup sliced fresh mushrooms
1 tablespoon oil

1 pound spaghetti or vermicelli

Sauce
⅓ cup oil
⅓ cup unbleached white flour
3 cups *White Wave* Silk Soymilk or reserved cooking water
½ cup chopped fresh parsley
1½ teaspoons salt
½ teaspoon garlic powder
⅛ teaspoon cayenne

Per serving: Calories 511, Total Protein 20 g, Soy Protein 11 g, Fat 28 g, Carbohydrates 46 g, Calcium 184 mg, Fiber 7 g, Sodium 1075 mg

STIR-FRIED PEAS AND TOFU

Yield: 4 to 6 servings

Preparation Time: 20 minutes

Children enjoy this mild, Cantonese-style dish made with ingredients that you probably always have in the house.

¾ pound *White Wave* **Reduced Fat Tofu**

1 tablespoon each nutritional yeast flakes, tamari, and dry sherry (or non-alcoholic alternate)

1 teaspoon cornstarch dissolved in ¼ cup cold water

1 teaspoon minced fresh gingerroot

2 cups frozen baby peas (petit pois)

1 cup low-salt vegetarian broth

3 tablespoons tamari

1 teaspoon sugar or alternate

4 teaspoons cornstarch dissolved in 2 tablespoons cold water

Cut the tofu into little squares, and toss in a bowl with the 1 tablespoon tamari, yeast flakes, and sherry.

Heat a medium nonstick skillet or wok over high heat, and brown the seasoned tofu. Add the ginger, peas, broth, 3 tablespoons tamari, and sugar. Simmer until the peas are just tender, then add the dissolved cornstarch. Stir over high heat until thickened, and serve with steamed rice.

Per serving: Calories 141, Total Protein 12 g, Soy Protein 9 g, Fat 3 g, Carbohydrates 17 g, Calcium 51 mg, Fiber 4 g, Sodium 809 mg

SWEET "CHEESE" AND PHYLLO TURNOVERS

Yield: 16 turnovers

Preparation Time: 20 minutes

Cooking Time: 15 to 20 minutes

These subtly sweet, but delicious, "cheese" pastries are usually made with a ricotta-like soft cheese and are deep-fried. They are just as scrumptious when a sweet tofu filling is substituted and encased in a crisply baked phyllo pastry.

The flavoring is orange blossom water, a flower extract that is used extensively in Middle Eastern cooking. It can be purchased in Middle Eastern or East Indian grocery stores, and some health food stores and pharmacies.

To make the filling, mix together the squeezed tofu, soymilk, sugar, orange blossom water, and salt in a medium bowl. Set aside.

To fill the pastries, stack the phyllo sheets together with the edges even. Cut with scissors into four 6 x 5-inch rectangles. Keep the rectangles well covered with plastic wrap while you work.

Preheat the oven to 400°F. For each triangle, place a heaping tablespoon of filling in the lower left-hand corner of one phyllo rectangle. (Have the 5-inch sides at the bottom and top.) Fold the right half of the rectangle over the left half, covering the filling. Now roll the filled end up, and keep folding over in this "flag" fashion, maintaining the triangle shape, until you come to the other end.

Place the filled triangles on lightly oiled baking sheets, not touching. Brush the tops with soymilk or apple juice concentrate, and bake for 15 to 20 minutes, or until golden and crispy. Place on wire cookie racks to cool. If they get soft when cooled, you can crisp them up in the oven again briefly.

8 ounces *White Wave* Reduced Fat Tofu, crumbled and squeezed in a clean tea towel

¼ cup *White Wave* Silk Soymilk (Organic Plain)

2 tablespoons sugar or alternate sweetener to taste

1 teaspoon orange blossom water

¼ teaspoon salt

4 whole sheets of phyllo pastry, thawed and kept covered

White Wave Silk Soymilk or thawed frozen apple juice concentrate for brushing tops

Per serving: Calories 36, Total Protein 2 g, Soy Protein 2 g, Fat 1 g, Carbohydrates 5 g, Calcium 6 mg, Fiber 1 g, Sodium 54 mg

TOFU PEASANT PIE

Yield: 6 to 8 servings
Preparation Time: 45 minutes
Cooking Time: 45 minutes

¼ cup tamari

2 tablespoons oil

½ teaspoon garlic powder

1 pound *White Wave* Firm Tofu, frozen, thawed, squeezed dry, and cut into bite-size pieces

2 cups chopped onions

½ pound mushrooms, sliced

2 cloves garlic, pressed

3 tablespoons oil

1 unbaked 9-inch deep-dish pie shell

2 tablespoons butter

¼ cup *White Wave* Silk Organic Plain Soymilk

6 medium potatoes, cooked and mashed

Salt and pepper, to taste

Combine the tamari, 2 tablespoons oil, and garlic powder, and pour over the thawed frozen tofu pieces. Marinate for at least 1 hour.

Sauté the onions, mushrooms, and pressed garlic in the 3 tablespoons oil until tender. Lightly brown the tofu and its marinade in another pan, then mix it together with the vegetables, and put them in the unbaked pie shell.

Preheat the oven to 375°F.

Whip the butter and Silk soymilk into the mashed potatoes. Stir in salt and pepper to taste. Spread the potatoes over the top of the pie, and bake for about 45 minutes until the filling is bubbly and the potato topping is browned.

Variations

You can add roasted garlic, White Wave Soy A Melt, or dairy cheese to the mashed potatoes for added flavor.

Per serving: Calories 421, Total Protein 12 g, Soy Protein 8 g, Fat 22 g, Carbohydrates 42 g, Calcium 126 mg, Fiber 5 g, Sodium 574 mg

TOFU SPINACH PIE

Yield: one 9-inch pie (6 to 8 servings)
Preparation Time: 10 minutes
Cooking Time: 30 minutes

Preheat the oven to 400°F.

Sauté the onions in the olive oil over low heat until soft. Add the tofu and brown. Add the spinach and sauté 2 more minutes.

Combine with the rest of the ingredients, mix well, and pour into the pie shell. Bake for about 30 minutes, or until the crust is golden.

1½ cups chopped onions

1 tablespoon olive oil

1 pound *White Wave* Soft Tofu, mashed or crumbled

1 (10-ounce) package frozen chopped spinach, thawed and drained,
or 1 pound fresh spinach, chopped

1 partially baked 9-inch pie shell

1 tablespoon lemon juice

1 teaspoon salt

½ teaspoon garlic powder

2 tablespoons dill seeds

¼ cup feta, crumbled (optional)

Per serving: Calories 233, Total Protein 10 g, Soy Protein 7 g, Fat 14 g, Carbohydrates 17 g, Calcium 145 mg, Fiber 3 g, Sodium 505 mg

57

BARBECUED SOUTHERN TEMPEH

Yield: 6 servings
Preparation Time: 20 minutes
Cooking Time: 2 hours

These tempeh strips in a tangy sauce will remind you of your favorite barbecue "ribs." Serve alongside potato salad or a colorful pasta salad. Any leftover barbecue sauce can be frozen in small containers for future use.

⅓ cup oil
¼ cup tamari
1½ tablespoons paprika
1 teaspoon granulated onion powder
½ teaspoon granulated garlic powder

1 pound *White Wave* Organic Original Soy Tempeh

1 medium onion, chopped
4 to 5 cloves garlic
⅓ cup oil
3 cups tomato sauce
½ cup water
¾ cup liquid sweetener
¼ cup molasses
½ cup Dijon mustard
1 teaspoon dried parsley
1 teaspoon salt
1 teaspoon allspice
¼ to ½ teaspoon crushed red pepper
½ cup lemon juice
2 tablespoons tamari

To make a marinade, combine the first ⅓ cup oil, the ¼ cup tamari, and the paprika, onion, and garlic powders until smooth. Cut the tempeh into narrow strips about 2 inches long and ½ inch thick. Place the strips in a metal, glass, or ceramic bowl, and cover with the marinade for at least an hour. Stir the strips occasionally so that all the sides will be coated.

Meanwhile, make the barbecue sauce by sautéing the onion and garlic in the remaining ⅓ cup oil in a large, heavy saucepan or stock pot until the onion is translucent. Add all the remaining ingredients, except the lemon juice and tamari, and bring to a boil. Reduce the heat to low, and simmer for 1 hour, stirring occasionally. Then add the lemon juice and tamari, and simmer for 10 more minutes.

Preheat the oven to 350°F.

Place the marinated tempeh strips on oiled baking sheets, and bake for 20 minutes on each side. Pour the barbecue sauce over the strips, and bake for 10 to 15 minutes more. Serve hot with your favorite barbecue side dishes, or chill for a picnic treat.

Per serving: Calories 580, Total Protein 19 g, Soy Protein 17 g, Fat 26 g, Carbohydrates 66 g, Calcium 68 mg, Fiber 10 g, Sodium 2682 mg

CHIP'S CHOP

Yield: 6 to 8 servings

Preparation Time: 25 minutes

Cooking Time: 25 minutes

If you have any leftovers of this delicious tempeh dish, they're great sliced in half lengthwise in a sandwich with lettuce, tomato, pickles, and horseradish.

Combine the water, yeast flakes, tamari, nutmeg, and granulated garlic and onion. Pour into a shallow pan, and add the tempeh pieces. Bring the mixture to a boil, and simmer for 15 to 20 minutes.

Meanwhile, combine the breadcrumbs, ground walnuts, and coconut (if using). Place on a dish for breading the tempeh. Pour the beaten eggs in a separate dish.

Preheat the oven to 350°F.

Dip the tempeh "chops" first in the beaten egg and then in the breading mixture. Place in a shallow, oiled baking dish, cover, and bake for 15 minutes. Turn the pieces over and bake uncovered for an additional 10 minutes.

Remove from the oven and serve with mashed potatoes and gravy.

2¼ cups water

¼ cup nutritional yeast flakes

1½ tablespoons tamari

¼ teaspoon nutmeg

½ teaspoon granulated garlic powder

½ teaspoon granulated onion powder

1 pound *White Wave* Organic Original Soy Tempeh, cut in triangles and sliced through widthwise

1½ cups breadcrumbs

1 cup ground walnuts

¼ cup flaked coconut (optional)

2 eggs, lightly beaten

Per serving: Calories 361, Total Protein 23 g, Soy Protein 14 g, Fat 17 g, Carbohydrates 30 g, Calcium 78 mg, Fiber 6 g, Sodium 400 mg

COUNTRY-STYLE TEMPEH WITH APPLESAUCE

Yield: 6 servings (12 patties)
Preparation Time: 15 minutes
Cooking Time: 20 minutes

1 pound *White Wave* **Organic Original Soy Tempeh, crumbled or grated**
¼ cup flour
1 tablespoon dried sage
¼ teaspoon ground nutmeg
¼ teaspoon ground allspice
¾ teaspoon dry mustard
¼ teaspoon crushed red pepper flakes
½ teaspoon black pepper
½ teaspoon dried marjoram
1 teaspoon salt

2-4 tablespoons oil

1½ cups applesauce

Combine all the ingredients (except the oil and applesauce) thoroughly in a bowl, then shape into 3-inch patties. Fry in the oil in a covered heavy skillet over medium heat until browned on both sides.

Warm the applesauce and serve alongside the tempeh patties.

Per patty: Calories 97, Total Protein 8 g, Soy Protein 8 g, Fat 3 g, Carbohydrates 10 g, Calcium 16 mg, Fiber 4 g, Sodium 178 mg

CREAMY GRAVY MUSHROOM STROGANOFF

Yield: 6 servings
Preparation Time: 25 minutes
Cooking Time: 20 minutes

I recommend this recipe for those new to tempeh, as the flavors are delightful.

Simmer the tempeh and bay leaf in the water for 15 minutes; drain. Cool and cut the tempeh into thin slices about 2 inches long. Sprinkle with the tamari.

Quickly sauté the mushroom slices in 1 tablespoon of the oil over medium high heat until they begin to brown and give out their juices. Place in a bowl. Brown the tempeh slices in 2 tablespoons of the oil, and add to the mushrooms in the bowl. Sauté the chopped onion in the remaining tablespoon of oil until soft. Sprinkle the onions with the arrowroot or cornstarch. Stir the hot vegetable stock in slowly. Cook this sauce about 5 minutes, until it thickens and bubbles. Reduce the heat and slowly stir in the sour cream. Add the mushrooms and tempeh to the pan to heat through, being careful not to boil the sauce. Serve over cooked noodles.

8 ounces *White Wave* Five Grain Tempeh, cut in half crosswise
1 bay leaf
1 cup water
2 tablespoons tamari
4 tablespoons oil
8 ounces mushrooms, sliced
1 cup chopped onions
2 tablespoons arrowroot or cornstarch
2 cups hot vegetable stock
½ cup soy sour cream, at room temperature

Per serving: Calories 214, Total Protein 8 g, Soy Protein 7 g, Fat 13 g, Carbohydrates 16 g, Calcium 20 mg, Fiber 3 g, Sodium 455 mg

MARINATED LEMON BROIL TEMPEH

Yield: 1½ quarts marinade (12 servings)
Preparation Time: 10 minutes
Marinating Time: 24 to 48 hours
Cooking Time: 15 to 20 minutes

Here is the recipe for the White Wave favorite, Lemon Broil Tempeh. We no longer make it, but we wouldn't want to deprive anyone of this delicious way to serve tempeh. This is enough marinade for four 8-ounce blocks of tempeh.

Lemon Marinade

1¾ cups water

1¾ cups soy sauce

1¾ cups olive oil

⅔ cup vegetable oil

¼ cup lemon juice concentrate

5 tablespoons granulated garlic

2½ tablespoons granulated onion

2 pounds *White Wave* Original Soy Tempeh

Combine all of the marinade ingredients, and stir well. Marinate the tempeh for 24 to 48 hours.

Preheat the oven to 425°F.

Place the marinated tempeh on a baking sheet, coat it lightly with the marinade, and bake for about 15 to 20 minutes, or until you have reached the desired crispness.

Per serving: Calories 331, Total Protein 18 g, Soy Protein 18 g, Fat 24 g, Carbohydrates 11 g, Calcium 24 mg, Fiber 6 g, Sodium 1005 mg

SALLY'S SLOPPY JOES

Yield: 6 servings
Preparation Time: 10 minutes
Cooking Time: 30 minutes

Looking for a ten-minute meal that tastes great? Here it is.

Sauté the onion and green pepper in the olive oil until soft. Cut the tempeh into chunks and process in a food processor. Add the tempeh to the onion and peppers, and stir. Add the rest of the ingredients, and mix well. Simmer and eat! This tastes terrific on whole grain buns.

A contribution by Sally.

1 medium onion, chopped
1 medium green bell pepper, chopped
2 tablespoons olive oil

1 package *White Wave* Organic Sea Veggie Tempeh or other *White Wave* Tempeh
½ cup water
1 tablespoon mustard
½ cup ketchup
1 tablespoon red wine vinegar
Salt, to taste

Per serving: Calories 219, Total Protein 10 g, Soy Protein 9 g, Fat 9 g, Carbohydrates 20 g, Calcium 25 mg, Fiber 7 g, Sodium 437 mg

SUKIYAKI WITH BROCCOLI AND CAULIFLOWER

Yield: 6 servings
Preparation Time: 25 minutes
Cooking Time: 10 minutes

A delightful Japanese medley of tempeh and vegetables.

8 ounces *White Wave*
**Organic Sea Veggie
Tempeh**

3 tablespoons tamari

2 tablespoons mirin

1 tablespoon arrowroot or
cornstarch

1 teaspoon vegetarian
Worcestershire sauce

1 teaspoon rice syrup or
maple syrup

1 cup vegetable stock

1 large carrot, cut into
matchsticks

1 cup broccoli florets

1 cup thinly sliced
cauliflower

1 tablespoon finely minced
gingerroot

1 green bell pepper, thinly
sliced

1 large onion, cut in thin
wedges

1 cup thinly sliced celery

¼ cup vegetable oil

2 tablespoons tamari

Steam the tempeh for 10 minutes, then cool and cut up into thin strips. Marinate in the 3 tablespoons tamari, the mirin, arrowroot or cornstarch, Worcestershire sauce, and rice or maple syrup. Stir occasionally so the tempeh is coated.

Bring the vegetable stock to boil in a saucepan. Add the carrot, broccoli, and cauliflower, and simmer for 1 minute only. Drain at once, reserving the liquid for the sauce. Drain the tempeh and add any remaining marinade to the vegetable liquid.

Sauté the tempeh slices in half the oil in a wok or large skillet until browned; set aside. Stir fry the onion and pepper for a few minutes in the remaining oil. Then add the celery, cook 1 minute, then add the carrots, broccoli, and cauliflower. Cook 2 minutes. Pour the liquid into the pan, bring to a simmer, then add the tempeh and the 2 tablespoons tamari to make a thin sauce. Serve at once over cooked rice.

Pictured at right:
Savory Tofu Spaghetti Balls, page 51

Per serving: Calories 195, Total Protein 8 g, Soy Protein 7 g, Fat 10 g,
Carbohydrates 14 g, Calcium 39 mg, Fiber 6 g, Sodium 879 mg

SWEET-SOUR TEMPEH KEBABS

Yield: 8 kebabs
Preparation Time: 20 minutes
Marinating Time: 2 to 24 hours
Cooking Time: 30 to 35 minutes

Cook these tangy, colorful kebabs in the oven or on the grill. Try mixing tempeh and frozen tofu to make these kebabs.

In a glass or stainless steel pan, spread out the vegetables and fruit one layer thick.

Whip together the marinade ingredients.

Microwave Method: In a glass bowl, microwave the marinade on high for 6 minutes, stopping to whip every 2 minutes.

Stovetop Method: In a saucepan, heat the marinade over medium heat, stirring constantly until it boils and starts to thicken. Reduce the heat and simmer for 2 to 3 minutes.

Pour the marinade over the vegetable chunks. Marinate in the refrigerator for a few hours to overnight.

Preheat the grill or oven to 400°F.

Arrange the tempeh and vegetables on skewers, then arrange on a pan or on the grill. Brush with the marinade and bake or grill for 15 to 20 minutes on each side or until browned. Serve the kebabs on a bed of brown rice, noodles, or millet. Heat the remaining sauce and pour over the top of the kebabs.

Pictured at left:
Half and Half Cheesecake, page 77

8 ounces *White Wave* **Organic Original Soy Tempeh, steamed and cut into ¾-inch chunks**

1 green bell pepper, cut into ¾-inch chunks

1 red bell pepper, cut into ¾-inch chunks

1 medium onion, cut into ¾-inch chunks

1 zucchini, cut into ¾-inch chunks

2 apples or star fruit, cut into thick slices

Marinade

1½ cups apple juice

6 tablespoons cider vinegar

¼ cup honey

2 tablespoons tamari

2 tablespoons grated fresh gingerroot

4 cloves garlic, minced

2 tablespoons cornstarch or arrowroot

Per kebab: Calories 163, Total Protein 7 g, Soy Protein 6 g, Fat 2 g, Carbohydrates 27 g, Calcium 24 mg, Fiber 4 g, Sodium 258 mg

SZECHUAN TEMPEH WITH ALMONDS

Yield: 6 servings
Preparation Time: 30 minutes
Cooking Time: 20 minutes

The secret of stir-frying is having all the ingredients ready in advance: the vegetables, the sauce, and the tempeh.

8 ounces *White Wave* Organic Original Soy Tempeh

1 cup almonds

1 large onion, thinly sliced in half moons

1 cup thinly sliced leeks, green and white parts

1 cup thinly sliced celery, cut on the diagonal

1 green bell pepper, thinly sliced

¼ pound snow peas, ends trimmed

2 teaspoons finely chopped fresh gingerroot

1 cup vegetable stock

¼ cup tamari

2 tablespoons mirin

1 tablespoon arrowroot or corn starch

1 teaspoon rice syrup or maple syrup

½ teaspoon Chinese 5-spice powder

¼ cup light sesame oil

1 teaspoon dark sesame oil

Preheat the oven to 350°F.

Steam the tempeh for 10 minutes; cool and cut into thin strips 1 inch long. Pour boiling water over the almonds, slip off the skins, and roast the almonds in the oven for about 10 minutes. Be sure to have all the vegetables cut and ready.

To make a sauce, combine the vegetable stock, tamari, mirin, arrowroot or corn-starch, rice or maple syrup, and 5-spice powder in a small bowl, and set aside.

Quickly sauté the tempeh strips in half of the light sesame oil and the dark sesame oil in a wok or large skillet over medium high heat until browned. Remove to a paper towel, and set aside. Add the remaining light sesame oil to the pan, and add the onion, leeks, celery, green pepper, and gingerroot. Stir fry a few minutes, then add the snow peas. Push the vegetables to one side of the pan, pour in the sauce ingredients, then stir the vegetables and tempeh strips into the sauce. The sauce will thicken quickly. Serve at once over hot rice or Chinese noodles.

Per serving: Calories 365, Total Protein 15 g, Soy Protein 9 g, Fat 25 g, Carbohydrates 20 g, Calcium 114 mg, Fiber 8 g, Sodium 745 mg

TEMPEH REUBEN

Yield: 4 servings
Preparation Time: 10 minutes
Cooking Time: 10 minutes

This hot sandwich is great for a Sunday afternoon or an evening meal. It's guaranteed to satisfy your doubting friends.

Cut the tempeh in half, and then slice each section to half its thickness. Pour the oil into the skillet, and coat the tempeh on both sides. Sprinkle with a dash of the onion and garlic powder, and sauté over medium-low heat until golden. Add the tamari and cook 1 minute more.

While the tempeh is browning, combine the Russian dressing ingredients.

Butter one side of the bread or toast. Build the sandwiches (with the butter side out) as follows: Russian dressing, tempeh, sauerkraut, and cheese. Sauté the sandwiches until the bread is golden brown.

8 ounces *White Wave Organic Original Soy Tempeh*
2 tablespoons olive oil
⅛ teaspoon onion powder
⅛ teaspoon garlic powder
1-2 tablespoons tamari

Russian Dressing
½ cup soy mayonnaise
¼ cup ketchup
1 teaspoon horseradish sauce
1 teaspoon chopped onion
½ teaspoon vegetarian Worcestershire sauce

4 slices rye bread
3 tablespoons softened butter
¾ cup sauerkraut, warmed
3 ounces Swiss cheese

Per serving: Calories 510, Total Protein 22 g, Soy Protein 13 g, Fat 32 g, Carbohydrates 32 g, Calcium 260 mg, Fiber 7 g, Sodium 1253 mg

TEMPEH STEW

Yield: 3 servings
Preparation Time: 10 minutes
Cooking Time: 25 minutes

*A hearty dinner that can be made in minutes. The aroma from the kitchen
will carry your family in for dinner. The vegetables in our recipe are
just a suggestion; add your own favorites.*

¼ cup chopped onions

3 carrots, sliced

2 tablespoons sesame oil

1 package *White Wave*
Organic Wild Rice Tempeh

2 red potatoes, cut into
pieces

8 mushrooms, sliced

¼ cup tamari

¼ cup water

½ cup apple juice

1 tablespoon grated fresh
gingerroot

½ teaspoon thyme

Pepper, to taste

Cook the onions and carrots in the
sesame oil over medium-high heat for 3
or 4 minutes. Reduce the heat and add
the tempeh, potatoes, and mushrooms.
Cook and stir for a few more minutes.
Add the remaining ingredients and bring
to a boil. Lower the heat, cover, and simmer for about 20 minutes. Add more
water or apple juice if the stew becomes
too thick. If the stew is too salty, you can
add water to taste. Serve over brown rice.

Per serving: Calories 370, Total Protein 12 g, Soy Protein 10 g, Fat 15 g,
Carbohydrates 45 g, Calcium 46 mg, Fiber 9 g, Sodium 1715 mg

FAST SEITAN MUSHROOM STROGANOFF

Yield: 4 to 6 servings
Preparation Time: 15 minutes
Cooking Time: 5 to 10 minutes

Serve this delicious "meaty" stroganoff over hot pasta, rice, or mashed potatoes. (Start cooking these first, because the stroganoff is very quickly made.) Serve with a salad on the side.

In a large, nonstick skillet, steam-fry the onion and white mushrooms until the onion starts to soften. Add the seitan and stir-fry for a few minutes. Add the tomato paste along with the wine.

Dissolve the soup mix in the boiling water, and add to the pan with the wine and mustard. Simmer over medium-low heat for 5 minutes.

In the meantime, if you have no "sour cream" on hand, blend the tofu, lemon juice, salt, and sugar in a food processor or blender until very smooth.

Add the tofu "sour cream" to the pan over low heat, stirring gently until heated through. Serve immediately.

Variation

Instead of seitan, you can use slices of marinated firm tofu.

For extra flavor, add the tomato paste to the onion and mushrooms, and stir over medium heat until the paste starts to brown. Then add the seitan.

1 large onion, thinly sliced
½ pound white button mushrooms, sliced
2 (6-ounce) packages *White Wave* Traditionally Seasoned Seitan
2 cups boiling water
1 (1-ounce) packet vegetarian dried onion soup mix
2 tablespoons tomato paste
3 tablespoons dry sherry plus 3 tablespoons water, or ⅓ cup dry white wine (or non-alcoholic alternative)
1 teaspoon dry mustard
Scant 2 cups tofu sour cream, or ¾ cup *White Wave* Reduced Fat Tofu
1½ tablespoons lemon juice
¼ teaspoon sugar
⅛ teaspoon salt

Per serving: Calories 171, Protein 21 g, Fat 4 g, Carbohydrates 12 g, Calcium 14 mg, Fiber 2 g, Sodium 568 mg

FOUR-WAY GLAZED SEITAN

Yield: 4 servings
Preparation Time: 10 minutes
Marinating Time: 2 to 24 hours (optional)
Cooking Time: 10 minutes

These delicious glazes turn humble seitan into company fare. They are reminiscent of Oriental-style barbecued "ribs." Serve them with steamed rice, in hot pita pockets, low-fat wheat tortillas, or Mandarin pancakes.

To make any of the sauces, combine the ingredients in a blender for a few minutes.

You can "quick-marinate" by cooking the seitan in the sauce for 5 minutes at a simmer.

If using later, marinate the seitan in the sauce or glaze of your choice for several hours or days in the refrigerator.

Otherwise, just mix the sauce with the seitan, and spread the mixture on 1 large or 2 smaller, nonstick or lightly greased cookie sheets. Place under the broiler, about 4-inches from the heat, and broil on one side for 5 minutes, or until slightly charred. Turn everything over with a spatula, and broil the other side for another 5 minutes, or until slightly charred.

If you prefer kebabs, thread the marinated seitan on bamboo skewers that have been soaked in cold water for 15 minutes, and grill, barbecue, or broil them until slightly charred on all sides. Use the remaining sauce to baste the kebabs. You can alternate the chunks with pieces of onion, green pepper, mushroom, pineapple, eggplant, etc.

Glazed Tofu Chunks or Strips

This makes either a great, quick appetizer with a toothpick in each cube, or threaded on bamboo skewers with pineapple and green pepper chunks. Or you can serve it as a main dish over rice, or in pita pockets or tortillas.

Simply cut a block of *White Wave* Fat-Reduced Tofu into small chunks or strips. Brown them on all sides in a nonstick skillet. (It's okay if they get slightly charred in places.) Then almost cover with some sort of sticky glaze or barbecue sauce. Use ¾ to 1½ cups of sauce for 12 to 14 ounces of tofu. Cook over high heat, stirring, until the chunks get saturated and a bit sticky with the glaze.

2 packages *White Wave* Chicken Style or Traditionally Seasoned Seitan

Korean Barbecue Sauce
½ cup tamari
¼ cup water
2 green onions, chopped
3 tablespoons sugar or alternate
2 tablespoons hulled sesame seeds
2 tablespoons cornstarch
2 large cloves garlic, peeled
¼ teaspoon black pepper

Black Bean Sauce
⅓ cup water
⅓ cup Chinese black bean sauce
3 tablespoons dry sherry or white wine
3 tablespoons vinegar
3-4 tablespoons liquid sweetener
6-10 cloves garlic, peeled
2 teaspoons cornstarch

Sherry Glaze
1 small onion, chopped
6 tablespoons water
6 tablespoons tamari
⅓ cup dry sherry
¼ cup Sucanat or brown sugar
1 tablespoon cornstarch
4 cloves garlic, peeled

Jalapeño or Hot Red Pepper Jelly Glaze
⅓ cup wine or juice
⅓ cup tamari
⅓ cup jalapeño or hot red pepper jelly
¼-⅓ cup light liquid sweetener
½ teaspoon garlic granules, or 2 cloves garlic, crushed

Korean Sauce Per serving: Calories 238, Protein 35 g, Fat 2 g, Carbohydrates 19 g
Calcium 60 mg, Fiber 2 g, Sodium 2251 mg
Black Bean: Per serving: Calories 241, Protein 32 g, Fat 0 g, Carbohydrates 25 g
Calcium 11 mg, Fiber 1 g, Sodium 244 mg

Sherry Glaze: Per serving: Calories 237, Protein 34 g, Fat 0 g, Carbohydrates 20 g
Calcium 25 mg, Fiber 1 g, Sodium 1745 mg
Jalapeño Glaze: Per serving Calories 313, Protein 33 g, Fat 0 g, Carbohydrates 40 g
Calcium 10 mg, Fiber 1 g, Sodium 1505 mg

GRILLED YAKITORI SKEWERS

Yield: 8 servings

Preparation Time: 25 minutes

Cooking Time: 7 to 10 minutes

Traditional yakitori are little skewers of chicken and chicken liver with a sticky, Japanese soy glaze. Here we do the same with chunks of seitan and mushrooms. You can purchase bamboo skewers in most large supermarkets or hardware stores, Oriental grocery stores, or cookware shops.

Yakitori Glaze

¾ cup tamari

4½ tablespoons sugar or alternate

¾ cup dry sherry, mirin, or non-alcoholic alternate

3 tablespoons cornstarch mixed with ⅓ cup cold water

16 bamboo skewers (soaked in water for 15 minutes)

1½ pounds *White Wave* Chicken Style Seitan, cut into 24 cubes

32 small, fresh button mushrooms (preferably brown ones)

16 green onions, trimmed to include only 3 inches of the green stems and cut into 1½-inch lengths

Mix the tamari, sugar, and wine. If you want to grill them right away, simmer the tofu cubes with the marinade in a nonstick or lightly oiled skillet on medium-high heat for about 5 minutes, to absorb some of the marinade.

If using later, refrigerate the seitan cubes in the marinade for several hours or days, stirring or shaking once in a while.

When ready to cook, thread the marinated cubes on the soaked skewers alternately with the mushrooms and green onion pieces. Each skewer should hold 5 seitan cubes, 3 mushrooms, and 3 green onion pieces. Two skewers will have 6 cubes each.

Pour the remaining marinade into a small pot, and add the dissolved cornstarch and water. Stir over high heat until the sauce thickens and boils.

Brush the skewers with the sauce, and grill or broil about 3 to 4 inches from the heat source until glazed and slightly charred on all sides, basting with the glaze when you turn the skewers. They will take only about 7 minutes to cook.

Per serving: Calories 202, Protein 18 g, Fat0 g, Carbohydrates 24 g, Calcium 76 mg, Fiber 10 g, Sodium 1866 mg

SARINA'S PEPPER STEAK

Yield: 3 to 4 servings
Preparation Time: 10 minutes
Cooking Time: 15 minutes

This simple, tasty recipe was contributed by a long-time vegetarian and White Wave customer, Sara B.

Stir-fry the seitan, onion, garlic, and peppers in the oil until the onion is transparent or until the peppers are at the desired consistency.

Dissolve the cornstarch and vegetable bouillon in the boiling water, and remove from the heat. Pour the mixture into the pan with the seitan, and stir. Serve over couscous, rice, or noodles.

1 pound *White Wave* **Traditionally Seasoned Seitan, sliced into thin strips**

1 onion, sliced

1 clove garlic, minced

2 red or green bell peppers, sliced into thin strips

Oil for stir-frying

1 tablespoon cornstarch

1 teaspoon vegetable bouillon

1 cup boiling water

Per serving: Calories 196, Protein 36 g, Fat 0 g, Carbohydrates 12 g, Calcium 14 mg, Fiber 2 g, Sodium 319 mg

VEGETARIAN SUKIYAKI

Yield: 4 servings

Preparation Time: 20 minutes

With a large electric skillet, you can cook this at the table in true Japanese style.

Sauce
¼ cup tamari
¼ cup sugar or alternate
½ cup water
2 tablespoons dry sherry or mirin

1 pound *White Wave* **Reduced Fat Tofu**
½ pound seitan, thinly sliced (optional)
8-16 large shiitake mushrooms, cut in half, or brown mushrooms, thickly sliced
1 (10-ounce) package fresh spinach leaves, well washed and sliced 1 inch thick
1 (8-ounce) can sliced bamboo shoots, rinsed and drained
1 bunch green onions, cut into 2-inch lengths, or 1 large white onion, sliced
¼ pound dried shirataki noodles, Oriental rice vermicelli, or bean thread (cellophane) noodles, soaked in warm water for 15 minutes, or 2 cups fresh bean sprouts

Have all of the ingredients arranged in piles on a platter when you begin.

Mix all the sauce ingredients in a small saucepan, and cook over medium-low heat while you prepare the other ingredients.

Heat a large, nonstick skillet or electric skillet. Cut the block of tofu in half horizontally, and brown the halves on both sides in the hot pan. Remove from the pan and slice the pieces about ½ inch thick.

Place the sliced tofu, seitan, mushrooms, spinach, and bamboo shoots (and the white onion, if you are using it instead of the green onions) in separate piles in the hot pan, and pour the sauce over it all. When the sauce is bubbling and the spinach begins to wilt, turn everything over, not mixing it. Make room for the green onions and soaked noodles, and cook for a few more minutes, until the spinach and mushrooms are cooked and everything is hot. Serve immediately with steamed rice.

Per serving: Calories 334, Total Protein 16 g, Soy Protein 14 g, Fat 5 g, Carbohydrates 54 g, Calcium 136 mg, Fiber 7 g, Sodium 1073 mg

Desserts

ALMOST NO-FAT BROWNIES

Yield: 16 bars

Preparation Time: 10 minutes

Cooking Time: 25 minutes

You can also make these delicious morsels with carob powder instead of cocoa.

1 cup Sucanat or sugar

4 ounces *White Wave* Reduced Fat Tofu

½ cup unsweetened cocoa or carob powder

½ cup water

4 teaspoons powdered egg replacer

1 tablespoon coffee or coffee substitute granules

2-3 teaspoons pure vanilla extract or liqueur

1½ teaspoons vinegar

⅓ cup unbleached flour

½ teaspoon salt

½ teaspoon baking powder

½ teaspoon baking soda

Preheat the oven to 350°F.

In a blender or food processor, mix the sugar, tofu, cocoa, water, egg replacer, coffee granules, vanilla, and vinegar until smooth.

In a medium bowl, whisk together the flour, salt, baking powder, and soda. Add the cocoa mixture and mix briefly.

Pour the mixture into a nonstick, lightly oiled or sprayed 7 x 11-inch or 8 x 8-inch cake pan, and spread evenly. Bake for 25 minutes. Cool on a rack in the pan, then cut into 16 bars.

Per bar: Calories 76, Total Protein 2 g, Soy Protein 1 g, Fat 0 g, Carbohydrates 15 g, Calcium 21 mg, Fiber 1 g, Sodium 100 mg

HALF AND HALF CHEESECAKE

Yield: one 8-inch cheesecake (8 servings)
Preparation Time: 10 minutes
Cooking Time: 45 minutes

Preheat the oven to 350°F.

Crumble the tofu into a medium mixing bowl, and whisk in the remaining filling ingredients until just combined. Purée in two batches in a blender or in a single batch in a food processor until completely smooth and creamy. Pour into the unbaked pie shell, and bake for about 45 minutes.

Cool and add sliced strawberries for garnish, if desired.

Filling

½ pound *White Wave* Firm Tofu

½ pound soy cream cheese

½ cup brown sugar

⅓ cup brown rice syrup or corn syrup

2 tablespoons lemon juice

1 teaspoon vanilla

Pinch of salt

1 unbaked 8-inch graham cracker crust

Strawberries, sliced, for garnish (optional)

Per serving: Calories 281, Total Protein 5 g, Soy Protein 4 g, Fat 13 g, Carbohydrates 36 g, Calcium 53 mg, Fiber 1 g, Sodium 222 mg

TOFU PUMPKIN PIE

Yield: 6 servings
Preparation Time: 15 minutes
Cooking Time: 60 minutes

1 pound *White Wave* Soft Tofu

1 cup *White Wave* Silk Soymilk (Plain or Vanilla)

⅛ teaspoon salt

3 teaspoons cinnamon

½ teaspoon ground ginger

3 cups puréed pumpkin

¼ teaspoon nutmeg

½ teaspoon allspice

½ cup liquid sweetener of your choice

1 egg

1 deep dish pie crust

Preheat the oven to 350°F.

Blend the tofu and soymilk until creamy. Combine with all the remaining ingredients, and mix well. Pour into the pie crust, and bake at for 1 hour, or until set.

Per serving: Calories 409, Total Protein 14 g, Soy Protein 9 g, Fat 15 g, Carbohydrates 55 g, Calcium 177 mg, Fiber 5 g, Sodium 87 mg

BROWN RICE TREAT

Yield: 3 servings

Preparation Time: 10 minutes

This healthy rice dish makes a simple, guilt-free dessert.

Mix all the ingredients together in a saucepan over medium heat, and bring to a simmer. Reduce the heat to low, cover, and simmer for about 10 more minutes, or until the liquid is absorbed.

1¼ cups *White Wave* Silk Soymilk

¾ cup instant brown rice

¼ cup golden raisins

1 teaspoon nutmeg

1 teaspoon ground cloves

Per serving: Calories 170, Total Protein 3 g, Soy Protein 3 g, Fat 1 g, Carbohydrates 34 g, Calcium 29 mg, Fiber 1 g, Sodium 42 mg

MICROWAVE TAPIOCA

Yield: about 6 cups

Soaking Time: overnight

Preparation Time: 5 minutes

Cooking Time: 10 minutes

Here is an old-time favorite prepared by an updated method.

Soak the tapioca in 1 cup soymilk overnight.

Pour 3 cups soymilk into a 2-quart glass bowl or measuring cup. Add the soaked tapioca and sweetener with a whip. Microwave on high for 6 minutes, and stir thoroughly with a whisk.

Microwave on high again for 2 minutes, whip, and microwave 2 more minutes. Don't let it boil over. Whip in the vanilla and pour into individual serving dishes or a serving bowl. Serve warm or chill and serve.

½ cup small or medium pearl tapioca

1 cup *White Wave* Silk Soymilk

3 cups *White Wave* Silk Soymilk

1½ cups sweetener of choice, or to taste

2 teaspoons vanilla

Per ½ cup: Calories 57, Total Protein 2 g, Soy Protein 2 g, Fat 1 g, Carbohydrates 10 g, Calcium 11 mg, Fiber 0 g, Sodium 32 mg

CHOCOLATE PUDDING OR PIE FILLING

Yield: 4 cups

Preparation Time: 10 minutes

Cooking Time: 5 to 10 minutes

Chilling Time: 3 hours

⅓ cup cocoa

¾ cup sugar

¼ teaspoon salt

¼ cup cornstarch (⅓ cup cornstarch if making a pie)

3 cups *White Wave* Silk Soymilk

3 tablespoons margarine

1½ teaspoons vanilla

Combine the cocoa, sugar, salt, and cornstarch, and mix well.

Then add the soymilk, whipping constantly. Bring this mixture to a boil over medium heat, still whipping constantly, then lower the heat and cover. Let boil gently for 5 to 10 minutes.

Remove from the heat and whip in the margarine and vanilla.

Pour into a bowl or baked pie crust, and chill.

Per cup: Calories 330, Total Protein 6 g, Soy Protein 5 g, Fat 11 g, Carbohydrates51 g, Calcium 36 mg, Fiber 3 g, Sodium 307 mg

VANILLA PUDDING

Yield: 4 cups

Preparation Time: 10 minutes

Chilling Time: 2 to 3 hours

¾ cup sugar

¼ cup cornstarch

¼ teaspoon salt

3 cups *White Wave* Silk Soymilk

¼ cup margarine

2 teaspoons vanilla

Combine the sugar, cornstarch, and salt in a medium saucepan. Gradually blend in the milk, stirring until smooth. Cover and cook over low heat, boiling gently for about 5 minutes. Remove from the heat, and blend in the margarine and vanilla. Pour into dessert cups or a baked pie crust, and chill.

Per cup: Calories 325, Total Protein 5 g, Soy Protein 5 g, Fat 13 g, Carbohydrates 48 g, Calcium 27 mg, Fiber 0 g, Sodium 338 mg

OLD-FASHIONED RICE PUDDING

Yield: 6 servings

Preparation Time: 5 minutes

Cooking Time: 2½ to 3 hours

*This traditional dish was always made without eggs;
it's basically a milk dish thickened with rice.*

Preheat the oven to 300°F.

Pour the soymilk, rice, sweetener, salt, and raisins into an oiled, 2-quart casserole.

Sprinkle the top of the mixture with the nutmeg or cinnamon.

Bake the pudding for 20 minutes, then stir. Bake uncovered for 2½ hours if made in a metal pan, 3 hours if baked in glass or ceramic. The pudding will seem a bit runny, but it will thicken up as it cools.

Serve plain or with fruit, fruit syrup, or maple syrup. You can add many optional ingredients to this basic recipe: vanilla or other extracts, rum or liqueurs, grated citrus zest, other dried fruits such as apricots, or ½ teaspoon coconut extract.

4 cups *White Wave* Silk Soymilk

¼ cup short grain brown rice

¼ cup granulated sweetener of your choice or Sucanat, or 3 tablespoons honey

¼ teaspoon salt

⅓ cup raisins or currants (optional)

Nutmeg or cinnamon

Per serving: Calories 115, Total Protein 5 g, Soy Protein 4 g, Fat 2 g, Carbohydrates 20 g, Calcium 24 mg, Fiber 1 g, Sodium 153 mg

BLACKBERRY SOY ICE CREAM

Yield: 5 cups

Preparation Time: 10 minutes

Freezing Time: per your ice cream machine

Always have your ice cream mix as cold as possible before putting into the freezing machine. Freezing time will vary, but generally it takes about 6 to 7 minutes per quart.

3 cups *White Wave* Silk Soymilk

1½ cups blackberries

1 cup sweetener of choice

1 tablespoon soy lecithin

⅛ teaspoon salt

Blend all the ingredients together in a blender until smooth and creamy, and freeze according to your ice cream machine instructions.

Per cup: Calories 270, Total Protein 4 g, Soy Protein 4 g, Fat 5 g, Carbohydrates 54 g, Calcium 213 mg, Fiber 2 g, Sodium 63 mg

HONEY BANANA SOY ICE CREAM

Yield: 5 cups

Preparation Time: 5 minutes

Chilling Time: per your ice cream machine

3 cups *White Wave* Silk Soymilk

1 large or 2 medium bananas

4-6 tablespoons oil

½ cup honey

Dash of salt

Blend all of the ingredients, and freeze according to your ice cream machine instructions.

Per cup: Calories 335, Total Protein 4 g, Soy Protein 4 g, Fat 15 g, Carbohydrates 46 g, Calcium 203 mg, Fiber 1 g, Sodium 10 mg

ORANGE SILK CREMECICLE

Yield: 4 cups

Preparation Time: 5 minutes

Chilling Time: per your ice cream machine

Combine in a blender and freeze according to your ice cream machine instructions.

3 cups *White Wave* Silk Soymilk

1 cup sugar

¼ cup oil

3 tablespoons frozen orange juice concentrate

1-2 teaspoons vanilla

Dash of salt

Per cup: Calories 421, Total Protein5 g, Soy Protein 5 g, Fat 15 g, Carbohydrates 66 g, Calcium 253 mg, Fiber 0 g, Sodium 10 mg

PEACHY SOY ICE CREAM

Yield: about 6 cups

Preparation Time: 10 to 15 minutes

Freezing Time: per your ice cream machine

Try this at the height of peach season when the fruit is at its sweetest and most plentiful.

Blend all the ingredients together in a blender until smooth and creamy, and freeze according to your ice cream machine instructions. If you prefer chunks of peaches, chop the peaches separately, and fold into the soymilk mixture just before freezing.

3 cups *White Wave* Silk Soymilk

1½ cups fresh or frozen peaches, sliced

1 cup sweetener of choice, or to taste

¼ cup soy oil (optional)

1 tablespoon soy lecithin

1 teaspoon vanilla

⅛ teaspoon salt

Per cup: Calories 198, Total Protein 3 g, Soy Protein 3 g, Fat 3 g, Carbohydrates 39 g, Calcium 18 mg, Fiber 1 g, Sodium 94 mg

SILK EGGLESS NOG

Yield: 3 cups

Preparation Time: 5 minutes

We know you will enjoy this tasty holiday drink.

3 cups *White Wave* Silk
  Soymilk (Plain or Vanilla)
¼ cup brown sugar
1 teaspoon vanilla
1 teaspoon rum extract
1 teaspoon nutmeg

Blend all the ingredients in a blender, and serve. Sprinkle additional nutmeg on top if you like.

Per cup: Calories 178, Total Protein 7 g, Soy Protein 7 g, Fat 3 g,
Carbohydrates 32 g, Calcium 342 mg, Fiber 0 g, Sodium 17 mg

VANILLA MILK SHAKE

Yield: 2½ cups

Preparation Time: 5 minutes

2 cups *White Wave* Silk
  Soymilk (Plain or Vanilla)
¼ cup sugar
2 tablespoons oil
2-3 ice cubes
1 teaspoon pure vanilla
⅛ teaspoon salt

Combine in a blender until the ice is well blended. Serve at once. For a thicker milk shake, blend in an extra cup of ice. Milk shakes can also be made by whipping soy ice cream and adding a touch of soymilk to thin it down.

Per cup: Calories 232, Total Protein 5 g, Soy Protein 5 g, Fat 12 g,
Carbohydrates 25 g, Calcium 25 mg, Fiber 0 g, Sodium 187 mg

YOGURT PIE

Yield: 8 servings
Preparation Time: 10 minutes
Chilling Time: 5 minutes

This is delicious and appealing decorated with fresh fruit, whipped cream, or nondairy cream.

Dissolve the agar flakes in the apple juice in a medium saucepan. Add the yogurt and combine well. Simmer for 5 minutes over medium heat, stirring constantly to avoid sticking and scalding. Remove from the heat and pour into the prepared pie shell. Let cool slightly, then chill in the refrigerator.

1 tablespoon agar flakes
⅓ cup apple juice
Three 6-ounce containers *White Wave* Dairyless Yogurt
1 prepared 8- or 9-inch pie shell

Variation

You can make a slightly less firm pie without the agar. Slowly heat the yogurt in a saucepan until boiling. Reduce the heat and simmer for 4 minutes. Pour into a prebaked pie shell and cool slightly. Chill in the refrigerator until ready to serve.

Per serving: Calories 155, Total Protein 3 g, Soy Protein 2 g, Fat 8 g, Carbohydrates 17 g, Calcium 97 mg, Fiber 0 g, Sodium 142 mg

WHITE WAVE PRODUCT INDEX

Use your favorite White Wave products in the following recipes.

Tofu
Firm Tofu
Chili Con Tofu with Beans 44
Fresh Shiitake Stir-Fry 45
Greek Salad 34
Half and Half Cheesecake 77
Lasagne with Tofu 47
Lemon Ginger Tofu or Tempeh 48
Minestrone Soup 28
Oven Fried Tofu 50
Savory Tofu Spaghetti Balls 51
Sizzling Savory Tofu Steaks 52
Spaghetti Primavera 53
Spinach-Pine Nut Salad 36
Tabouli 37
Taco Salad 38
Tofu Pasta Salad 39
Tofu Peasant Pie 56

Reduced Fat Tofu
Almost No-Fat Brownies 76
Eggless Tofu Salad 22
Hawaiian Sticky Tofu 46
Light and Easy Corn Muffins 16
Mattar Tofu 49
Seitan Mushroom Stroganoff 69
Stir-Fried Peas and Tofu 54
Sweet "Cheese" and Phyllo Turnovers 55
Vegetarian Sukiyaki 74

Soft Tofu
Eggless Tofu Salad 22
Picnic Potato Salad 35
Scrambled Tofu Wrap 17
Tofu Pumpkin Pie 78
Tofu Spinach Pie 57

Baked Tofu
Jalapeño Mexican Style
Taco Salad 38
Sesame Peanut Thai Style
Oriental Pasta Salad with Peanut Sauce 42

Silk Soymilk
Blackberry Soy Ice Cream 82
Brown Rice Treat 79
Chocolate Pudding or Pie Filling 80
Eggless Blueberry Muffins 18
Herbed Oatmeal Scones 19
Honey Banana Soy Ice Cream 82
Microwave Tapioca 79
Old-Fashioned Rice Pudding 81
Orange Silk Cremecicle 83
Peachy Soy Ice Cream 83
Silk Eggless Nog 84
Soy Crepes 20
Spaghetti Primavera 53
Sweet "Cheese" and Phyllo Turnovers 55
Tofu Peasant Pie 36
Tofu Pumpkin Pie 78
Vanilla Milk Shake 84
Vanilla Pudding 80

Tempeh

Five Grain Tempeh

Creamy Gravy Mushroom Stroganoff
61

Organic Original Soy Tempeh

Barbecued Southern Tempeh 58
Chip's Chop 59
Country-Style Tempeh with
  Applesauce 60
Marinated Lemon Broil Tempeh 62
Phyllo Triangles with Tempeh Filling
  23
Sweet-Sour Tempeh Kebabs 65
Szechuan Tempeh with Almonds 66
Tempeh Chili 30
Tempeh Reuben 67
Vegetable Soup Provençale 31

Organic Sea Veggie Tempeh

Sukiyaki with Broccoli and
  Cauliflower 64
Sally's Sloppy Joes 63

Organic Wild Rice Tempeh

Tempeh Stew 68

Soy Rice Tempeh

Indonesian Cauliflower and Noodle
  Soup 29
Lemon Ginger Tofu or Tempeh 48
Spinach Mushroom Salad 40

Seitan

Chicken Style Seitan

Chicken-Style Salad 41
Grilled Yakitori Skewers 72

Traditionally Seasoned Seitan

Fast Seitan Mushroom Stroganoff 69
Sarina's Pepper Steak 73
Stuffed Mushrooms 25

Chicken Style or Traditionally Seasoned Seitan

Four-Way Glazed Seitan 70
Spring Rolls 24

White Wave Dairyless Yogurt

Yogurt Pie 85

INDEX

A

Almost No-Fat Brownies 76
Almonds, with Szechuan Tempeh 66

B

Barbecued Southern Tempeh 58
Blackberry Soy Ice Cream 82
Blueberry Soy Muffins, Eggless 18
Broccoli and Cauliflower Sukiyaki 64
Brown Rice Treat 79
Brownies, Almost No-Fat 76

C

Cauliflower and Broccoli Sukiyaki 64
Cauliflower and Noodle Soup, Indonesian 29
Cheesecake, Half and Half 77
Chicken-Style Salad 41
Chili Con Tofu With Beans 44
Chili, Tempeh 30
Chip's Chop 59
Chocolate Pudding or Pie Filling 80
Corn Muffins, Light and Easy 16
Country-Style Tempeh with Applesauce 60
Creamy Gravy Mushroom Stroganoff 61
Cremecicle, Orange Silk 83
Crepes, Soy 20

D

Dairyless Soy Yogurt
  Yogurt Pie 85

E

Eggless
  Blueberry Soy Muffins 18
  Silk Nog 84
  Tofu Salad 22

F

Four-Way Glazed Seitan 70

G

Ginger Lemon Tofu or Tempeh 48
Glazed Seitan, Four-Way 70
Gravy, Creamy Mushroom
  Stroganoff 61
Greek Salad 34
Grilled Yakitori Skewers 72

H

Half and Half Cheesecake 77
Hawaiian Sticky Tofu 46
Honey Banana Soy Ice Cream 82

I

Ice Cream
  Blackberry 82
  Honey Banana 82
  Peachy 73
Indian, Mattar Tofu 49
Indonesian Cauliflower and
  Noodle Soup 29

K

Kebabs, Sweet-Sour Tempeh 65

L

Lasagne with Tofu 47
Lemon Broil Tempeh, Marinated 62
Lemon Ginger Tofu or Tempeh 48

M

Marinated Lemon Broil Tempeh 62
Mattar Tofu 49
Microwave Tapioca 79
Milkshake, Vanilla 84
Minestrone Soup 28
Muffins, Eggless Blueberry Soy 18
Muffins, Light and Easy Corn 16
Mushroom
  Spinach Salad 40
  Stroganoff, Creamy Gravy 61
  Stroganoff, Fast Seitan 69
  Stuffed 25

O

Oatmeal Scones, Herbed 19
Orange Silk Cremecicle 83
Oriental Pasta Salad with Peanut
  Sauce 42
Oven Fried Tofu 50

P

Pasta Salad with Peanut Sauce,
  Oriental 42
Pasta Salad, Tofu 39
Peachy Soy Ice Cream 83
Peanut Sauce, with Oriental Pasta
  Salad 42
Peas and Tofu, Stir-Fried 54

Peasant Pie, Tofu 56
Pepper Steak, Sarina's 73
Phyllo Triangles with Tempeh
  Filling 23
Phyllo Turnovers and Sweet
  "Cheese" 55
Pie
  Chocolate 80
  Tofu Peasant 56
  Tofu Pumpkin 78
  Tofu Spinach 57
  Yogurt 85
Pine Nut-Spinach Salad 36
Potato Salad, Picnic 35
Provençale, Vegetable Soup 31
Pudding
  Chocolate 80
  Old-Fashioned Rice 81
  Vanilla 80
Pumpkin Pie, Tofu 78

R

Reuben, Tempeh 67
Rice Pudding, Old-Fashioned 81

S

Sally's Sloppy Joes 63
Sarina's Pepper Steak 73
Scones, Herbed Oatmeal 19
Scrambled Tofu Wrap 17
Seitan
  Chicken-Style Salad 41
  Fast Seitan Mushroom Stroganoff
  69
  Four-Way Glazed Seitan 70
  Grilled Yakitori Skewers 72
  Sarina's Pepper Steak 73

(Seitan, cont.)
  Spring Rolls 24
  Stuffed Mushrooms 25
Shiitake Stir-Fry, Fresh 45
Silk Eggless Nog 84
Sizzling Savory Tofu Steaks 52
Sloppy Joes, Sally's 63
Soy, about 9
Soy Crepes 20
Soy Muffins, Eggless Blueberry 18
Silk Soymilk
  Blackberry Soy Ice Cream 82
  Brown Rice Treat 79
  Chocolate Pudding or Pie Filling
    80
  Eggless Blueberry Muffins 18
  Herbed Oatmeal Scones 19
  Honey Banana Soy Ice Cream 82
  Microwave Tapioca 79
  Old-Fashioned Rice Pudding 81
  Orange Silk Cremecicle 83
  Peachy Soy Ice Cream 83
  Silk Eggless Nog 84
  Soy Crepes 20
  Spaghetti Primavera 53
  Sweet "Cheese" and Phyllo
    Turnovers 55
  Tofu Peasant Pie 56
  Tofu Pumpkin Pie 78
  Vanilla Milk Shake 84
  Vanilla Pudding 80
Spaghetti Balls, Savory Tofu 51
Spaghetti Primavera 53
Spinach
  Mushroom Salad 40
  Pine Nut Salad 36
  Tofu Pie 57

Spring Rolls 24
Stew, Tempeh 68
Stir-Fried Peas and Tofu 54
Stir-Fry, Fresh Shiitake 45
Stroganoff, Creamy Gravy
  Mushroom 61
Stroganoff, Fast Seitan Mushroom
  69
Sukiyaki with Broccoli and
  Cauliflower 64
Sukiyaki, Vegetarian 74
Sweet "Cheese" and Phyllo
  Turnovers 55
Sweet-Sour Tempeh Kebabs 65
Szechuan Tempeh with Almonds
  66

T

Tabouli 37
Taco Salad 38
Tapioca, Microwave 79
Tofu
  Almost No-Fat Brownies 76
  Chili Con Tofu with Beans 44
  Eggless Tofu Salad 22
  Fast Seitan Mushroom Stroganoff
    69
  Fresh Shiitake Stir-Fry 45
  Greek Salad 34
  Half and Half Cheesecake 77
  Hawaiian Sticky Tofu 46
  Lasagne with Tofu 47
  Lemon Ginger Tofu or Tempeh 48
  Light and Easy Corn Muffins 16
  Mattar Tofu 49
  Minestrone Soup 28
  Oriental Pasta Salad with Peanut
    Sauce 42

(Tofu, cont.)
Oven Fried Tofu 50
Picnic Potato Salad 35
Savory Tofu Spaghetti Balls 87
Scrambled Tofu Wrap 17
Sizzling Savory Tofu Steaks 52
Spaghetti Primavera 53
Spinach-Pine Nut Salad 36
Stir-Fried Peas and Tofu 54
Sweet "Cheese" and Phyllo
Turnovers 55
Tabouli 37
Taco Salad 38
Tofu Pasta Salad 39
Tofu Peasant Pie 56
Tofu Pumpkin Pie 78
Tofu Spinach Pie 57
Vegetarian Sukiyaki 74
Tempeh
Barbecued Southern Tempeh 58
Chip's Chop 59
Country-Style Tempeh with
Applesauce 60
Creamy Gravy Mushroom
Stroganoff 61
Filo Triangles with Tempeh Filling
23
Indonesian Cauliflower and
Noodle Soup 29

(Tempeh, cont.)
Lemon Ginger Tofu or Tempeh 48
Marinated Lemon Broil Tempeh
62
Sally's Sloppy Joes 63
Spinach Mushroom Salad 40
Sukiyaki with Broccoli and
Cauliflower 64
Sweet-Sour Tempeh Kebabs 65
Szechuan Tempeh with Almonds
66
Tempeh Chili 30
Tempeh Reuben 67
Tempeh Stew 68
Turnovers, Sweet "Cheese" and
Phyllo 55
Vegetable Soup Provençale 31

V

Vanilla Milk Shake 84
Vanilla Pudding 80
Vegetable Soup Provençale 31
Vegetarian Sukiyaki 74

W

White Wave products, about

Y

Yakitori Skewers, Grilled 72
Yogurt Pie 85

THE BEST TASTING SOYMILK IN THE DAIRY CASE

- Lactose Free
- 3 Flavors
  Vanilla
  Chocolate
  Plain
- Cholesterol Free
- Low 1% Fat
- Made from
  Organic Soybeans
- Silk™ is the
  fresh one
- Silk™ is Soy.

White Wave

America's Soy Food Company

Organic Silk™ Soymilk
•
Organic Tofu
•
Organic Baked Tofu
•
Organic Silk™ Yogurt

Some of the recipes in this book have come from the cookbooks below. They are available from your local bookseller, or you can order them from:

Book Publishing Company
P.O. Box 99
Summertown, TN 38483
1-888-260-8458

Please add $2.50 per book for shippping.

By
Louise Hagler

Tofu Cookery - $15.95
Tofu Quick & Easy - $9.95

Lighten Up! - $11.95

**Soyfoods Cookery
$9.95**

**The Almost No-Fat Holiday Cookbook
$12.95**

**20 Minutes to Dinner
$12.95**

**The Almost
No-Fat
Cookbook
$12.95**

By Bryanna Clark Grogan

Some of the recipes in this book have come from the cookbooks at right. They are available from your local bookseller, or you can order them from:

Book Publishing Company
P.O. Box 99
Summertown, TN 38483
1-888-260-8458

Please add $2.50 per book for shippping.

New Farm Vegetarian Cookbook - $9.95

Cooking with Gluten and Seitan $7.95

The Tempeh Cookbook $7.95

Also enjoy these fine vegetarian cookbooks from Book Publishing Company.

The TVP® Cookbook $7.95

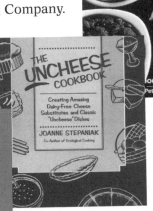

Tofu & Soyfoods Cookery $12.95

The Uncheese Cookbook $11.95

**Tollfree Ordering
1-888-260-8458**